Answer

Katie is nearly seve
school. Questioned by a 'do-good socia
herself re-living the past. Where did all the trouble start? Katie remembers the shock of the discovery that she was an adopted child ... the bitter resentment she felt at her foster-mother's re-marriage. She looks back at her desperate search for her 'real' mother — a search that led her to visit a famous actress in hospital, to track down a mysterious writer and finally to clash with the police. *Answering Miss Roberts* is tense, true-to-life ... the story of a girl today.

TOPLINERS

Answering Miss Roberts

Christopher Leach

MACMILLAN

For all the Katies

All the characters in this book are imaginary, and bear no relation to any person living or dead.

330 02175 3

First edition 1968
Reprinted 1971, 1972

Published by
MACMILLAN EDUCATION LTD
Basingstoke and London
The Macmillan Company of Canada Ltd, Toronto
The Macmillan Company of Australia Pty Ltd, Melbourne
St. Martin's Press Inc. New York
Companies and representatives throughout the world

Printed in Great Britain by
RICHARD CLAY (THE CHAUCER PRESS) LTD
Bungay, Suffolk

1

When we met outside the station I thought you were going to be different. I thought *Well, she's young enough* — and I liked that blue coat and the way you did your hair. You drove well, too. I've always admired people who seem to do things without effort.

And you were silent. I liked that. No chat about the weather, the condition of the countryside, what were my interests; no sugar over why I was there, and what I had done, the trouble I had been in; no avoiding the fact of where we were bound — that I was the prisoner and you the gaoler, and that the flat fields could have been the moon or the whole empty universe for all they meant to me. No escape: the hedges made of iron, and the grass shouting as soon as I touched it. You never said a word, and I thought you were going to be different from the others.

But this morning, when you gave us our assignments, I knew you were the same as every teacher, headmistress, professional do-gooder who ever interfered in my life.

Myself — A Teenager.

Why don't you just leave it alone, Miss Roberts? Why not just live your own life? Surely you have your own hopes and ambitions? You ask me to write the same essay as everyone else, and, like them, you expect the truth. But it's impossible. If you don't know that — then it's time you grew up. I'll only tell you what I think you want to know. I'll delight in giving you what you expect — except the truth. For behind my face, behind these words, I am as different again: untouched, undissected. I am myself.

In five months' time I shall be seventeen — but I'm no teenager. I refuse to be lumped with anyone. All I want is to be left alone. I want an end to probings, to talks on sex and grooming and posture, and life.

But, Miss Roberts, since you've asked . . .

My real life began when I was nine years old. Before that it was all imaginary, an acting-out, a playing the part of a daughter in a small house in a small village in Somerset.

I learned to read early and, when my mother wanted me for anything, the first place she'd look was in the branches of the elm in the field at the end of her garden. I can still see her looking up, her face half-hidden by the pages of my book.

It was here that she came, a few days after my ninth birthday.

'Katie!'

At other times I would have taken no notice: gone on reading another page at least. It was usually only an errand; a call to lunch or tea. But now she had only to call once — for it was almost a scream. My heart lurched, and I soon reached the grass.

She was dressed to go out, but with no handbag. Her usually relaxed face tight.

'Go and sit with Mrs. Hervey for a while,' she said. 'Hurry. I'll come and collect you later.'

I followed her through the clusters of seeding dandelions.

'Is it her leg again?'

'Just you go.'

Outside the gate a police-car waited. The one sitting beside the driver got out and opened the door for her. I must have guessed something, because I ran forward.

'Can I come? Please?'

She turned and looked at me, but it was plain I could have been the gate or the post-box for all the recognition in her eyes.

'Tell Mrs. Hervey I'll be along as soon as I can.'

The door slammed; the car slid away and gathered speed. Across the street Mrs. Jackson lifted her window and called.

'What's the matter, Katie?'

'I don't know.'

And I ran to the end of the street, across the bridge; and pulled the cord in the centre of the green paint-blistered door. Inside, in the clock-ticking dark of the living-room, she stirred in her armchair. The cat watched me from the valley of her lap.

'It's Katie, Mrs. Hervey.'

'I must have dozed off,' she said. 'Your mother with you?'

'No,' I said. 'She's gone in a police-car.'

'Off you get, Tiger,' she said, and slowly pushed herself upright. 'In a *what*, my love?'

I repeated it.

'Where's my stick? I always seem to ... Ah, thank you, dear. Now why should she go off in a police-car? Shall we have a cup of tea?'

I did my usual job automatically: filling the kettle, setting the tray with the large white cups, the milk-jug, the sugar in a glass bowl. Emptying the teapot. My mind elsewhere: in the speeding car; the question-mark at the end.

She, too, had done her part: four biscuits in the middle of the yellow plate. She held the other two in her hand.

'Will your mother be coming?'

'She won't be long,' I said, more out of hope than knowledge.

'Good,' she said. And the two joined the four.

We sat in opposite armchairs, waiting for the

kettle to boil. The cat rubbed itself against my legs, then gathered itself and jumped.

'You won't stay there long, Tiger,' she said. 'Perhaps she's helping them or something, Katie. Your mother, I mean. I shouldn't worry, dear.'

'She looked so . . .'

And I fought the tears clotting my voice.

'There, there,' she said. 'We'll have a nice cup of tea, and then . . .' She looked around. '. . . and then we'll have a look at my old album. I always said I'd show it to you one day, didn't I?'

At any other time it would have seemed funny: the two of us sitting on the lumpy sofa, the cat between us, the stiff paper brushing its nose, its paw sneaking out to halt a picture, its deep rumbling purr a constant background to her voice — a voice alive with memory.

'. . and here's our first house, Katie.'

Her finger moved, caressing the brown poplars.

'Lovely trees. Many's the time I've lain awake listening to them howling in the wind. So tall they were. Gone now. My Bertie took me back there a few years ago. Big main road there now. Terrible . . . And here *is* Bertie, in his pram.'

I looked at the baby squinting at the sun. Why a police-car? What had . . .? Had she done something? Why had she looked so . . .?

'And here he is again. Growing up. A baby one

minute, and then . . . He was ten then, I think. Yes, ten. Not much older than you, Katie. And nearly twelve here, when we all went to Hastings. That's his dad with him.'

'They look alike,' I said, for something to say, bored as I was with the caught waves, the caught clouds, the stiff smiles, the squat sandcastle with its little flag, the proud father with his own spade.

'Now isn't that funny you should say that, Katie,' she said, in some way delighted. 'I always said so myself. There's one of them together up here . . . Here, see? Now don't they look alike? As if he was our own son.'

'Oh?' I said, interest reviving. 'Wasn't he really, then?'

'No,' she said. 'He was my sister's boy. She died having him, and his father went back to Canada. Blessing in a way — seeing I couldn't have any myself. No, we brought him up as our own. Not official like, not like your mother adopted you. I always thought that we . . .'

She talked on, unaware of the explosion.

'I wasn't adopted,' I said.

'Yes you were, dear,' she said, her voice abstracted, her attention still on the photographs. Then, half-realizing the situation, she looked at me. Something in my face increased her embarrassment. 'I . . . I always thought you were adopted, Katie. Perhaps I'm wrong, dear. Yes, I'm sure I am. Getting you mixed up with someone else — that's what I'm doing.'

'Susan Poole's adopted,' I said.

'That's who it must be then,' she said. 'Now, this is where we lived before we came here. Looks nice, doesn't it? But that thatch! Beetles and spiders and . . .'

We spent the next half hour with the album. Yet I think we both knew we were merely pretending — covering the damage with laughter at the old cars and fashions.

The one question I wanted to ask my mother wilted on my lips when she finally returned. She had put on fresh make-up. I smelled the powder as she bent and kissed me and pulled me to her. But her face was different.

'Your father's had an accident, Katie,' she said. 'That's why I had to go in the . . .'

'Oh, my love,' said Mrs. Hervey. 'I'll put the kettle on.'

'No, we must be going,' said my mother. 'Thank you for looking after her.'

'Is he hurt bad?' she said.

'I'm taking you to your Aunt Mary's,' said my mother. 'We'll have to hurry to get the train.'

'*Is* he bad?' I said.

'Yes,' she said. 'He is.'

The day of the funeral I was left in my aunt's

house with my cousin Hilary. She was about sixteen then, and resented having to spend the morning with me. In the end we went our own ways: she to her record-player, and I into the garden with a magazine.

It was a beautiful Spring day: sunlight, the blossom brilliant on the two apple-trees near the fence. There was an old iron seat seemingly rooted into the earth, surrounded by daisies. I put the magazine on the peeling slats and sat down.

Above me the blossom lifted itself to the sun winking between the shifting branches. I had loved my father. If anyone had had to go, I would have preferred it be my mother. It was a hard thought, or wish, but it was true. He was gentle and imaginative. He needed no book to read to me at bedtime — for months he had continued the story of the two horses that had run away from their master and travelled the world. Dumpling and Debbie — the adventures of. He had encouraged me to read all and everything. Loving poetry, he had communicated the same love to me.

'You've got your father's mind,' she had said once. 'You don't know the difference between lying and exaggeration.'

I still had not asked her whether or not I had been adopted. But, again, I felt it to be true.

Perhaps every child wonders if he or she really came from the people they call their parents. One of my great dreams when I was about seven was that I was of noble birth, born of some great person whose fortune would be lost if my existence were known. And that eventually he or she — usually she — would stand at the door with all the necessary papers, behind her the Rolls-Royce and the chauffeur, a tartan rug draped over his arm. And the news would be broken to me (news I had known for years but never spoken of), and the woman who had posed as my mother until then would ask in a broken voice if she might be allowed to visit us, and my real mother — she of the grey fur and the expensive gloves — would say *It is up to Melanie* (which was my real name) and I would look down at her in the chair by the fire and say yes. And then the long drive to a house strangely like the one I'm in now — and the servants and my own suite of rooms and the private governess and the holidays in Switzerland . . .

Born with perhaps more imagination than was good for me I would draw clues from the fact that I did not share the fairness of my mother and father — I was dark, with brown eyes, whereas she was mousy and he several shades lighter. I loved the country, but longed for a life comparable to that which I found in books. I half-wished for terrible accidents involving my parents — sudden, painless deaths — which would cause the grey-haired solicitor to reveal his secret long before I was twenty-one.

And now one of them *was* dead. And in an accident. Sitting there on the thin magazine, feeling the hard slats through the pages, I saw the tractor toppling, heard the shouts, and the sudden silence. Somewhere beyond the apple-trees they were burying him — and, although he was not my real father, I wept.

She came for me after tea — a tea I had helped Hilary prepare, keeping my head down to hide my raw face.

'Thank God you've only got her, Alice,' said my aunt, changed now from her black, cool in a blue dress, her arms full-fleshed. 'Still, you'll have to get a job now, love, I suppose.'

'Yes,' said my mother. 'There won't be much. It won't last us long. I'll have to look around.'

She was quiet all through the journey home. Full of grief myself, imagining the empty house, I still could not ask her about my real parents. I told myself, as the telegraph-poles and the farms and the cattle raced in the opposite direction and the wires rose and fell to my breathing, that I would leave the questions until another day: when she was more settled. I sensed the gap in both our lives, and, during the following weeks, I behaved as best I could; though often, and unknown to her, I would wake in the night to discover tears sliding off my face and onto the pillow.

But, as time went on, she could not settle. She missed him too much. Returning from school at the end of the day I would hear, as I entered, the sewing-machine whirring in the living-room, and find yet another new dress begun or finished; or discover her still busy about the house, polishing furniture she had polished the day before. Originally from Bristol, she had borne the rural life for his sake, but now she began to dislike the village, wanting to make a new beginning. She felt the call of the city — of noise and of crowds.

And so it was, not six months after his death, that we moved to London, to a flat in Fulham — and she returned to nursing.

Although I was lonely at first away from the few school-friends I had had in the village, I found London exciting enough. The parks were a poor substitute for the fields I had left, but there were visits to the Zoo and the galleries and the museums. Best of all was the local library. Starved of choice as I had been at home — the grey van calling once a week and the same titles staring back — the large modern building was a treasure-house.

Gradually the ache subsided. There were days when I forgot him entirely — only to suddenly remember his face or a phrase he often used, and to feel that I had somehow let him down.

And then, in the holiday between leaving Primary School and going to the Grammar, my mother took me once more to the West End. But this time for a different reason.

2

Looking back on it now, six years later, I realize I should have known. Or at least guessed. But when, as we waited for the bus, I asked her again where we were going — for never before had everything I wore been completely new — and she said, also once again, *You'll see,* I visualized nothing more unusual than a theatre matinee, rather than a wearying trudge round the stores; a trip on the river and a meal at some waterfront hotel, than a cupped hand feeling the cold claws of hungry pigeons.

We got off the bus at Hyde Park Corner, and my mother looked at her watch. I felt the excitement in her, and I responded.

'Oh, where are we going?' I said. 'Tell me.'

'Let's walk down Piccadilly,' she said. 'We don't want to be too early.'

An unusually soft smile warmed her face, and in that instant I felt closer to her than I had ever been. It was not love — I hoarded that for my real mother — but it was as near as I could make it. I took her arm, and for that long walk did not look into everyone's eyes, searching for recognition, but concentrated on the rich shops ablaze with cars and jewellery and leather-bound books, and the sliced bodies of aeroplanes in which sat miniature passengers bound for nowhere.

At the Circus she looked again at her watch.

'We took longer than I thought,' she said. 'We'll have to get another bus.'

'Where to?'

'Trafalgar Square,' she said. 'Here's one.'

My heart chilled.

'Not the pigeons?' I said.

She laughed and smoothed back hair from my forehead.

'No, silly,' she said. 'Not the pigeons. In those clothes?'

'Not there?' I said as we passed the National Gallery.

'No,' she said. 'Now you just wait.'

We got off the bus, crossed near the station, and stopped outside the Corner House. In the large mirror near the entrance I saw our twin magnificence reflected: her glowing red coat, the white glare of my gloves.

We waited.

'Are we meeting someone?'

'Yes.'

'Who?'

She looked left towards the Square, then right

towards the station, her face a little flushed, her teeth biting her lip.

'You'll see.'

'Aunt Mary?' I said. I hoped it wasn't.

'No.'

'Has Mrs. Jackson come up?'

'Katie, please. You'll soon . . .'

She stopped. And waved.

He came towards us. He was very dark. What I would call Italian-looking. But not flashy. And under the natural darkness of his face was a paleness that appeared bruise-coloured around his nostrils and beneath his eyes. He gave the impression of wanting to hurry, but not being able to. The colour of the flowers he was carrying sang against his dark suit: vivid red roses.

'Alice,' he said, and bent to kiss her. She deflected her face — because of me, I suppose, but I had not missed the attempt, the assured familiarity — and stood behind me.

'This is Katie,' she said.

His hand was hard over my glove, and I almost cried out.

'Well, well,' he said. One of his teeth was silver. It glinted wetly above his tongue. 'Pleased to meet you, Katie.'

'This is Mr. Morris, Katie,' said my mother. 'Where are the boys? I thought you were . . .'

The roses rustled in their white funnel as he waved his hand.

'They send their apologies, Alice. They wanted to come . . . but they're on some run down to the coast or somewhere. Another day they'll meet Katie. Eh, Katie?'

There was nothing I could say.

'Mr. Morris has two sons,' she said. 'One's just left school, this term.'

'Oh?' I said.

'These are for you, Alice,' he said. They seemed to enter my mother — the same red as her coat. As she began to thank him he took the square box from under his arm and held it out.

'And this for you, Katie.'

Through the thin tissue I could read the name of the chocolates, see the pale yellow ribbon like a sunny river or a vein of gold.

'Thank you.'

The silver tooth glinted.

'Good,' he said. 'That's a weight off my mind — *and* my hands.'

My mother gave the expected laugh.

'Shall we, then?' he said.

And we entered the Corner House.

'And when they brought you in you did look a mess.'

He peered up from lighting his cigar, the flame reddening his hand.

'And look at me now,' he said. 'Steady as a rock.' The match burned upright and firm for a second, then trembled. 'All due to good nursing. Your mother's a real Florence Nightingale, did you know that, Katie? Queen of Alexandra Ward, that's what she is.'

'You weren't a very good patient, anyway,' she said.

'I'll say I wasn't. I . . .'

'Anything else, sir?' said the waitress.

'Yes, I'd like a brandy if it's possible. *And* — in a brandy glass. And make it two. No, don't argue, Alice. You do what you're told. Or shall we say three, Katie? Ha. Now, what was I saying? Oh yes. Patients. My word, that Sister Kendrew — what a witch she was. Remember when you were changing my dressing that morning and she . . .'

I looked from one to the other, there in my new dress stiff against my legs, my new shoes pinching a little, the thin half-heard music coming from somewhere above my head — and I knew my life was going to change, *had* changed the second she had stopped in mid-sentence and waved; and he had stepped forward.

The brandy arrived and he cupped his hands around the fat glass.

'Well, here's to us, Alice — and Katie. You know,

I'm very fond of your mother, Katie.'

'Jack,' she said. 'Jack . . . I don't think I want this. Really. You finish it.'

'Sure?' he said. 'Good stuff.'

He poured hers into his glass.

'Yes,' he said, 'I'm sorry the lads couldn't have been here. They wanted to meet you as much as I did, Katie. I tell you what, Alice: why don't we all meet on Sunday, the five of us, and go out into the country for a run?'

'I'm sorry,' she said. 'I'd like to — but I'm on duty. At least until late.'

'Pity,' he said. He looked down into the remains of his brandy. 'What about just Katie, then?' His eyes met mine. 'Just the four of us. Get to know each other better, wouldn't we?'

'Yes,' said my mother, 'why don't you, love? You look a bit pale. Get some sea-air into your lungs. I'm sure the boys . . .'

'I can't,' I said. 'Don't you remember? I'm having tea with Mr. Marshall.'

'Are you?' she said. 'It's her old headmaster, Jack. The school she's just left. Very impressed with her English, wasn't he, Katie? You didn't tell me you were going.'

'Yes I did. I've got to be there at four. Sheila's going, too.'

'Ah well,' he said. He finished his brandy. 'Another time, eh?'

I think I disliked him at sight. Anyway, that's what I tell myself now. I disliked his assurance, his easy way with my mother. He had none of Dad's shyness, none of his quiet. Like a steamroller he crushed all resistance. He organized outings, met me outside the school and drove me to places he said I'd like — and some I would have done if it had not been he who had taken me.

Over the next few weeks I met his sons. The younger, Frank, I liked; but Greg, now free of school, was set for bigger things than his father's new woman, and if forced to come on the same excursions as all the others — the unchanging countryside with its clusters of cows and horses, the shamble of houses bleached by the elements as the coast was neared, the walks on the piers, the darkened amusement-arcades — he was all boredom and sullenness, and finally stopped coming altogether.

Of course, Mr. Marshall had not asked me to tea that Sunday. I had to find an excuse. It was true he had liked my essays — I still remember being asked to stand while he commented on one to the rest of the class — but he stayed remote in his pipe-smelling study. No, I used that afternoon for another purpose.

That same morning I had walked through the bell-beating Sabbath sunlight to warn Sheila. She stood at the door as I began to explain.

'Who is it?' her mother called.

'Katie. I'm going out for a minute.'

'Don't you go far. Dinner's early today, remember.'

We crossed the road to the recreation-ground, sat on one of the seats, and watched the tennis-players as we talked.

'We're going out ourselves this afternoon,' she said. 'Supposing your mother meets mine and asks?'

'You know there's not much chance of that,' I said — 'the hours she does. Go on — all I'm asking you to do is say we went and had a good time. The usual.'

'I don't know,' she said. Then she looked up from considering her fingernails. 'Oh all right. I suppose so.'

I thanked her. We stood up and wandered over to the wire-mesh fence and rested our fingers on the white metal.

'What will you do, anyway?' she said. 'This afternoon, I mean?'

'I don't know,' I said. 'I'll think of something.'

She looked at me. Very carefully.

'What's the matter?' I said, as the silence lengthened.

'Do you know Eva Stewart?' she said.

'No,' I said. 'I don't think so. Whose class was she in?'

Sheila laughed.

'She's a film-star, dope. You don't go to the pictures much, do you?'

'Not much. Still, she can't be much of a film-star if I haven't heard of her. Oh, wait a minute . . . No, I don't think it was her. Why, anyway?'

'There's a picture of her today in the paper. My mother saw it first. *Doesn't she look like Katie?* she said. And Dad and me looked. You do, you know. A bit. When she was younger, of course.'

'What paper?' I said.

'*The People*. Do you have that?'

'No.'

'You ought to see it. Like you — really she is.'

'Wait a minute.' I dug my hand into my coat-pocket. 'I thought so — I've got a shilling here. Let's go to Stone's and get one.'

The paper bought, I opened it outside the shop.

'What page?'

'Somewhere near the back. You know — films and all that.'

And it was like looking at an adult version of myself. *Eva Stewart returns to filming after a long absence. To star in new version of Lorna Doone.*

'Doesn't she, though?' said Sheila.

'Yes.'

'Told you.'

As we walked back to her house I could not help but look again and again.

'How old do you think she is?' I said.

'Don't know. Thirty, about? It says after a long absence. Wonder why?'

Her mother opened the door.

'Good girl,' she said. 'Almost ready.'

'Katie's seen that one of Eva Stewart.'

Her mother laughed.

'No relation, is she?' she said.

That afternoon, while my mother was at the hospital, I did what I had planned to do.

Ever since my half-guessed difference had been confirmed by Mrs. Hervey's slip of the tongue, I had longed to find some proof, some document which would release me from my family, make the dream tangible. And so I began the search.

For more than an hour I went over the whole flat like a detective. I found nothing that surprised me: it was the usual mess of doctors' cards and reminders and lists and old bills. From the living-room to her bedroom; to the tins in the kitchen which, empty, breathed herbs and spices; to even the bathroom-cabinet whose mirror, once I had closed the door, reflected only my disappointment.

Then I remembered the suitcases under her bed. There were two; the larger contained old woollens; cardigans, berets, scarves. The other . . . was locked.

I sat on the carpet and considered where the keys might be. Perhaps in the mother-of-pearl jewel-box on the dressing-table? But there were only a few brooches and earrings. Returning, I tested the catches again. Firm and strong. I lifted the case on the bed and turned it over. The underside was rubbed and scored with use, and one of the corner-strengtheners was loose, a loop of thread caught in one of the studs. I found that if I pulled the thread the whole of the bottom creaked, and in the widening gap I caught a glimpse of white. I got a knife with a sharp point, and carefully teased out the thread, until half of that side was free. By pulling hard I made the gap wide enough for my hand to enter. Almost sick with excitement and fear, my heart thumping and my throat dry, I brought out, piece by piece, what was inside.

Insurance forms. A batch of letters from my father, held by a thick elastic band. Their wedding-certificate. A pile of photographs — mostly of me, from the cradle to a year or so back. A pair of long white gloves. And an envelope with almost a hundred pounds in fivers.

Nothing else. No stunning revelation. No proof. Nothing. The only spark being the *absence* of my birth-certificate. I put everything back, pressed the gap home, looped the thread once again over the stud, and slipped the case under the bed.

In the living-room I looked at the clock. She would be home in about two hours. I picked up the paper and studied Eva Stewart's face. Then I found a writing-pad and envelope, and wrote a letter.

Dear Eva Stewart,

I have seen your picture in today's People. *I have seen all your films and think you are a marvellous actress.*

Could you please send me a signed photograph of yourself? And could you tell me how old you are, and if you are married? And why it has been such a long time since we have seen you?

I am looking forward to seeing your new film.

Yours sincerely,
Katie Gilson

I addressed the envelope 'care of' the studios, and took a stamp from the book on the sideboard. I ran down the stairs and posted it in the box on the corner. Back again in the flat I carefully cut out her picture and pasted it on a piece of card, and put it in the drawer of the table by my bed.

Then I turned on the television, and watched until I heard her key in the door.

3

Completely new things make me uncomfortable. This applies to situations, people before they become friends; clothes and objects. The exception is books, possibly. Yet there is something about very old books. I once discovered one on a stall in Soho: an old guide to morals printed in seventeen-twelve; and on the flyleaf was a signature and a date. I've never forgotten that pale brown faded name: *Anne Marsh 1760*. I couldn't afford to buy it, but stood there with the thin pages crackling in my hands, the smell of age blurring those of petrol and oil — the calm face in the mind's eye: *Anne Marsh*.

No, I like things when they've been used a little; when you can relax, take off the mask — or at least wear another nearer the truth. When the shine has gone the shoes stop pinching.

But the next few days after writing to Eva Stewart were full of newness, and I grew irritable and tired. I started at the Grammar School: new faces, new teachers, new uniform, new rules, new buildings, new status. Towards the end of the week I began to feel better, although the Sixth Form were still giants and the assembly-hall like a hangar.

With all this newness I had almost forgotten the letter, and for the past two evenings had not considered her face before sleep. But, that Friday, the large envelope was there, next to the fruit-bowl. One of the oranges had fallen off the pile, and, where the afternoon sun struck, it cast a warm bloom on the white square.

'Letter for you,' she called from the bathroom.

'Yes, I've seen it.'

The name of the studios in pale blue above my name.

She came in as I was opening it.

'Going into films, Katie?'

I did not look up, but I was conscious of her perfume — something she had never used before, but now wore often.

The stiff cards held a thin sheet between them. Her glossy face met mine, and again it was like holding a mirror which unaccountably added a few years to the onlooker's reflection.

'Who's that?' she said, and came closer.

'Guess.'

She took it from my hand.

'Oh, it's . . . it's Eva Stewart, isn't it? Did you send for it?'

'Don't you notice anything?'

'No,' she said. 'Oh, the resemblance, you mean?

Yes, you do look a little like her. Is that why you . . .? *To Katie Gilson*. Signed, too. And is that a letter?'

'Yes.'

'Well, let's hear what she says.'

I took the picture from her hand, put it and the letter back between the covers, and into the envelope.

'It's for me,' I said.

She cocked her head at me.

'You *are* a funny girl sometimes, Katie. Now, come and have your tea.'

'What time will you be home?' I said.

'Oh, not late. I'm bringing Mr. Morris back for coffee. You'll be all right, will you? Why not ask Sheila round after all. I do think you . . .'

'No, I'll be all right,' I said. 'I'll go to the library and change my books. Oh, and can I have some money, please? One of them is overdue.'

She tucked the silk scarf into her collar and reached for her handbag.

'You're sure now?' she said. 'You can always go and see the Wheelers, you know. She was saying only the other day that you . . .'

'I'll go to the library,' I said, slowly. 'And then I'll watch the play. Don't worry.'

'How do I look?' she said, turning in a circle. 'Will I do?'

'Yes.'

She came closer and cupped my face in her hands.

'You're always so serious, Katie. What's the matter? The new school not what you . . .'

'I'm just a bit tired.'

'At your age? Why, I remember how I used to . . . Well, I suppose it *is* a strain. Come on, give me a smile. That's better.'

She kissed me. The tiny grains of powder around her nose.

'Do you think you'll find some friends at school?' she said. 'Someone you can invite home, and go out with? I sometimes feel you're too much alone.'

'Then I ought to have had some brothers and sisters then, hadn't I?'

Her face clouded — and I was sorry.

'Yes, it might have been better, Katie. But we can't have everything we want. World's not made like that. Look after yourself, dear. And get the coffee-things ready for about half-past nine.'

After she had gone I went to my room. Above the mantelpiece was a framed piece of embroidery I had done years ago. I unclipped the back, took out the cloth, cleaned the glass and tried her photograph. It was a little too big and I had to trim it before it fitted. Finally it rested on the table, tilted against some paperbacks, and her face watched me as I read her letter. It was typed and bore the studio letter-head.

Dear Katie Gilson,

Miss Stewart was very pleased to receive your letter, and she was most interested in what you had to say.

In answer to your questions she is

(1) *twenty-nine years of age and*

(2) *is unmarried.*

(3) *She has been very ill, but has now recovered.*

She hopes you will like her new film, and she has pleasure in sending you a signed photograph.

Yours faithfully,
Margaret Cox (Miss)
Reliance Studios

I looked carefully at the photograph. The dedication and the signature were in different inks, and the former looked very much as though Miss Cox had written it.

I tore the letter twice and dropped the pieces into the waste-bin near my bed. I was tempted to do the same with the photograph — but instead I gathered my library books together and left the flat.

Mrs. Wheeler was coming up the stairs with her shopping. She puffed to a halt.

'Hallo, Katie. More reading? You ought to get a bit of sun, girl. Is your mother out?'

'Yes.'

She clicked her tongue.

'Well, come and have some tea . . .'

'I've just had it,' I said.

'Well,' she said, 'if you get lonely you come in.'

'I never get lonely,' I said.

She sighed.

'Then you're lucky, Katie. Very lucky, my girl.'

On the way to the library I checked once more the other titles of Richard O'Dell. I had just read, and re-read, his *The Answer*. It had hit me like a thunderbolt — this story of a sculptor's life from poverty to a kind of fame, and then the clash with the authorities over his commission for a memorial to the war dead; his integrity, their refusal, his untimely death; and the work finding a home in the Tate. This was the book which was overdue, and even now I half-regretted returning it — intending to renew it if none of his other titles were on the shelves.

But once there, the fine paid, I found another: *Boy Pan*. It had a marvellous dust-jacket: a suburban garden, looking up towards a typical semi-detached; a greenhouse; flower-pots, hollyhocks, a tangle of weeds — the whole ordinariness transformed by the strange blue-grey colouring, and the face half-seen in the foreground: a face seemingly composed of leaves, only the eyes human. On the back was a photograph of the author: a lean, angular man, his hands linked on a low wall, behind him what looked like the Mediterranean, sunlight on white walls.

On the way home my anger at Eva Stewart lessened. I began to find reasons for the impersonality of the letter. Of course, she must get thousands; she couldn't answer them all personally; she was too busy. She must have read mine, at least. And perhaps she had wondered who Katie Gilson was . . . Yet, underneath all these excuses, the fake dedication rankled.

When I got to the flat I saw that there was an hour to wait before the play began; so I turned on the radio, found some music and settled down to the book.

Once again I was held. The story was of a boy born to normal parents, but who, at an early age, began to show a preference for the company of animals and birds, and who liked to sleep outside the house in a tent at the end of the garden. As time went on he found he could communicate with all kinds of non-human life, even at the lowest level: could sense the world of the ant and the moth, be at one with the thrush and the blackbird, his humanity sloughed off like another skin. Until one day he could no longer hear the voices of his parents, could not . . .

'Katie, love.'

I looked up. They were standing near the chair, smiling.

'Sorry,' I said. 'I didn't hear you come in.'

'That must be quite a book,' he said.

'It is.' I stood up. 'I've forgotten to get the coffee ready.'

'I can see that,' she said. 'I'll do it. Sit down, Jack. Turn that off, if you like.'

'No, I like this kind of music,' he said. 'Can I help?'

'You just take it easy.'

I followed her into the kitchen and began to set the cups on the trolley.

'Did you have a good time?'

She half-turned, the spoon deep in the coffee-tin.

'Lovely.'

Still bemused by the book, I seemed to sense a difference in her, too. Her face was flushed and her eyes overbright.

'Yes, we had a lovely meal, and then we walked through Green Park to the car. I'll finish that, love. Go and keep Mr. Morris company.'

He was sitting on the sofa, my book in his hands.

'Do you like this, Katie? Really?'

'Yes.'

He shook his head.

'Not my kind of thing at all. I never did like the . . . the fantasy kind. Not that I read a lot, anyway. Don't seem to get the time any more.' He closed it, put it down, and leaned back, his hands behind his head. 'Well, how are we, Katie?'

'All right, thank you.'

'Like your new school?'

'Yes.'

'What are you going to do afterwards? Got any ideas?'

'I don't know,' I said. 'I think I'd like to be a writer.'

I was as surprised as he — it was as if a deeper me had spoken of a dream I myself had not realized.

'A writer!' he said. 'Of what?'

The deeper me shrank before his mocking smile.

'Oh . . . poetry, perhaps.'

'Hear that, Alice?' he called. 'Your daughter wants to be a poet.'

She came in and ruffled my hair.

'Well, why not? She's written some nice ones in her time, haven't you? And Mr. Marshall always said she . . .'

'We'll have to see what we can do, then,' he said. 'Got any of them handy? Your poems, I mean?'

Surprised at his interest, I hesitated.

'There's some around, I suppose.'

'Well then, we'll have to see them one day, won't we?'

She went back into the kitchen. There was a short silence. The radio tinkled a waltz. He looked at me, critically.

'A poet, eh?'

She came back, wheeling the trolley. He stood up. Again I sensed something, I didn't know what.

But I knew soon enough.

I put the cup back carefully, forcing my attention on the need not to spill the coffee, and away from my suddenly weak limbs.

'When?' I said.

'Oh, not for a while yet, love.'

'Can't come too soon for me,' he said, sitting on the arm of the sofa and squeezing her shoulder. 'I'd do it tomorrow — if your mother agreed. But she says it'll take time for you to get used to the idea. Will it, Katie?'

I moistened my dry mouth.

'Well, aren't you going to congratulate us, anyway?' he said.

She reached over and put her hand on my knee.

'Poor Katie, it's a shock, isn't it?'

I couldn't think straight. Part of me wanted to scream. I thought wildly of the years ahead: with him and his sons, the eternal car-trips to the coast; moving into that big house in the North End Road.

'Why?' I said. 'Why do you want to . . .?'

'Why?' he said, and gave an unfunny laugh. 'Because we love each other — that's why. Why else do people get married?'

I looked at her.

'Because they're lonely, sometimes.'

'No, I love Jack, Katie. Really I do. Think of all

the fun we can have together. You'll have those brothers you wanted.' How could she be that stupid? 'I know we're going to be happy.'

He picked up his cup and looked at me over the rim.

'You don't dislike me, Katie, do you?'

I saw my father sitting in his place, and the contrast was too great.

'Excuse me,' I said, and walked slowly to my room.

'It's all right,' I heard her say. 'Leave her.'

A few minutes later I heard the door open and close, and felt the bed give as she sat down beside me.

'I'm sorry, Katie. I should have prepared you. But I do love him.'

'How can you?' I said. 'After Dad. How can you love someone like that?'

'Don't you want me to be happy, pet?' she said. 'I know he's not your real father, but . . .'

'Real father?' I almost shouted. '*Real* father?' I sat up. 'Neither was Dad, was he? I'm not *your* pet, either, am I? You're not my real mother, are you? I was adopted, wasn't I? Wasn't I?'

And still I couldn't cry, although a rough heat burned behind my eyes.

She tried to put her arms around me, but I wriggled free and went and stood near the window. Down below cars passed, and I thought how strange that other people should be going somewhere while all this was happening to me.

There was a quiet knock at the door.

'All right?' he said, without opening it.

She turned slowly, as if her head were very heavy.

'I'll be out in a minute, Jack,' she said.

She came and stood next to me.

'I'll see Jack out, and then we can have a long talk. I should have done it years ago.'

I didn't answer, but part of me suddenly sang with what I can only call happiness, or perhaps even ecstasy. *It was true . . . it was true.*

Then who was I, really?

I heard them talking for a minute, heard him say *You're sure now? You're sure?* And then the front door closing, the silence and her return.

'Come into the other room,' she said.

I looked back at Eva Stewart.

'I'm all right here.'

'No, I can't talk in there, Katie. Come out. Please.'

She patted the space on the sofa, and I sat next to her, but not touching. And it was she who was trying to keep the tears away.

'When did you guess?' she said.

And I told her all my dreams; of my darkness and their fairness — and of poor old Mrs. Hervey.

'Your father always wanted to tell you,' she said, twisting the handkerchief in her hands. 'Don't be sad, Katie love. It doesn't make any difference, honestly it doesn't, dear. You're still my daughter. And isn't it nice to know that you were chosen and needed? You see, I . . .'

'Who am I?' I said.

'You're Katie Gilson. That's what you were at six weeks old, and that's what you'll stay. Although it'll soon be Katie Morris, won't it? You see, love, what happened was this . . .'

'Is my real mother alive? Is she?'

She sighed.

'Let me tell it my way, dear. It's as much a trial to me. Coming on top of everything else: Jack, and everything. You see, I did have a baby, once. Your father and me. A girl. She died just after she was born. And it seemed there was a chance I might not have any more. We wanted you very much, Katie.'

'You wanted someone,' I said. 'Not me.'

'Once we had you, we loved you like our own. You couldn't have been loved more, dear.'

'Who was she?'

'We never knew, Katie. We didn't know then, and I certainly don't know now. It was for the best, Katie. Better she didn't have any idea, and that we didn't, too.'

'Why didn't you tell me?'

'I was going to — often. So was your father — but I said wait. I kept putting it off. I suppose I was afraid . . . afraid of losing you. Then he died, and that made it worse. You were all I had left. But I'm glad you know now: we can both start afresh. Can't we, Katie?'

She sounded so despairing that I instinctively reached out a hand. She took it as though it were a lifeline.

'I know we'll be happy, Katie,' she said. 'I won't have to work when I'm married, and that means we can spend more time together again. I haven't been a bad mother, have I? Not treated you so badly?'

All she had done for me over the years finally released my own tears, but I was hard and stiff in her arms.

And later that night, as the rest of the world swished by in the rain, I lay awake, fitting faces and houses and streets and cities to that other woman who perhaps also lay awake, equally wondering, equally aching for certainty.

4

They were married three months later: months in which I had tired her first to irritation and then to anger with my questions.

'All right,' I said one day when we were packing. 'I won't ask any more, if you'll just answer one.'

'That depends,' she said, wrapping newspaper around another cup and putting it in the tea-chest. 'I might.'

'Promise you'll answer, and I'll promise not to ask any more.'

'All right.' She held the next cup still. 'Go on. But this is the last. Remember.'

'What was the name of the Society?'

She reached for another piece of newspaper and made a great bustle as she wrapped.

'I've told you time and time again, Katie, that I'm not going to tell you that. You know I won't. So why keep on asking?'

'You promised.'

'You knew I wouldn't tell you — so what's the use?'

'Then my promise doesn't count either.'

She rested her hand on the straw.

'Don't you realize how much this hurts me, Katie? Of course it's natural for you to want to know about your mother. But if *I* don't know, how can you find out? Please, Katie, I know I should have told you years ago. But don't spoil everything — just when I could be really happy.'

'You won't tell me? Ever?'

'No, Katie.' She was very calm and determined. 'You're my daughter. Your own mother didn't want you. No, I'm sorry, dear — perhaps *couldn't* have you, keep you. But I've brought you up, and it hasn't always been easy. I think I deserve some thanks and some consideration. Now, I don't want to hear any more of it. Help me carry this over there.'

But a clue came at the reception.

It was held at a small hotel not far from the Registry Office. There were relatives from both sides, and some of his business friends: he ran a car-hire firm.

And towards the end of the morning, just before they left for Paris and we were farmed out until the following Monday, the noise grew louder, almost drowning the music of the trio in the corner; the pile of empty champagne bottles grew higher; faces redder, and their owners friendlier.

She came out of a cluster of laughing men, and made towards me.

'You look warm, Aunt Mary,' I said.

She plumped down in the other chair.

'Hold this for me will you, dear?'

I took the glass and waited as she mopped her face with a small blue wispy handkerchief.

'Ooh, it is hot in these places,' she said. 'I'll have it back now. Have you had any of this?'

'At the toast,' I said. 'I don't like it. Tastes like vinegar.'

'That's a good girl,' she said. 'You stick to your orange-squash.' She emptied her glass and held it cradled in her lap. 'Your mother's done well for herself, Katie. Nice husband, nice big house, nice pair of boys.' She laid her hand on my arm. '*And* a nice daughter too, of course.' She leaned closer and studied my face. 'I hear you know all about it now. Being adopted.'

'Yes.'

Her fingers squeezed.

'It's best in the long run. Not too much of a shock, was it? I remember the day you arrived home. You *were* made a fuss of. You were lucky, Katie. You could have done a lot worse.'

I saw my chance, and spoke very casually.

'Yes, Mum told me all about it. How the Society wouldn't let her know who my real mother was.'

'I wonder if there's any more of this?' she said,

looking round. 'I expect some more'll be along in a minute. Yes, they have to be very careful. She might have wanted you back one day. And you wouldn't have liked that. Very particular, they are. Thinking of you *and* her, really.'

'Does every Society do that? Not just the one Mum went to?'

'I think so, dear. Ah, here's the man I've been waiting for.' The waiter filled her glass. 'Thank you.'

'How did she find the one I came from?'

'Oh, I think she contacted some vicar or other. He must have put her on to them. Through the Church, or something. I remember how tired they were — both your Dad and your Mum — when they got you home. Tired, but happy.'

'Do you think that if I wrote a letter to them — to the Society, I mean — thanking them for finding me such a good home, they'd be pleased?'

It took her breath away. Her eyes widened.

'Why, what a lovely idea, Katie. Yes, why don't you do that, dear? I'm sure they'd appreciate it. Nice for your mother to know too. Yes.'

'Now what was the name again, Aunt Mary? I could easily find the address in the phone-book.'

'Oh, I don't know, dear. You'll have to ask your mother.'

'Yes, I will. You don't remember, then?'

She puckered her forehead as she sipped.

'So long ago. It was something to do with Saint Michael, I think. Somewhere near Victoria. Yes, you write to them, Katie. What a nice idea.'

And I did just that — although I hadn't intended to. It was easy to find in the phone-book, still with an address in Victoria. I wrote and thanked them. And, as a sort of off-hand postscript, I asked if they could possibly tell me where I was born, and anything about my real mother.

I half-expected the answer, yet hoped for something more. The letter came a day or so after they had returned from Paris, and I remember racing up the stairs in that tall dark house and sitting on the unmade bed to read it. They thanked me in return, said it was rare to receive such a letter; but, they were sorry, details such as I requested were never divulged. Good luck and God bless you.

'Who was that from?' she said, as I sat down to breakfast.

'Oh, nothing much. Just something I sent off for.'

'I thought it must have been one of your poems accepted by the *Sunday Times* — the way you shot up the stairs,' he said. 'I still haven't seen any, by the way.'

'You want to get yourself a fella, Kate,' said Greg. 'Write a lot of poems then, you will.'

'Plenty of time for that,' she said. 'Isn't there, Katie?'

'Never too early to start,' said Greg. 'Eh, Dad?'

'I wouldn't know about such things,' said his father; and they both laughed.

I think it was the combination of the letter, and his guess that I might be sending out some of my poems, that made me send the story to *Beatrice* — you know the magazine, Miss Roberts.

They ran a competition every month that readers could enter — something that had to be based on actual experience. Mine wasn't, but once I thought about the idea for a while I decided to send it anyway, and take a chance. In a way it *was* based on experience: an experience I had lived through day after day, and night after night. I told the story of a girl who discovers she is adopted, and who tries to find her real mother. Unlike me, she was successful — but here is the strange thing — in my story there was no rich figure in grey fur, no Rolls, no chauffeur with a tartan rug, no white mansion at the end of a long cedar-lined drive. The mother turned out to be dull and weary with child-bearing, living on a noisy council estate, dressing for the evening's bingo session, smoking like a chimney; and, final reality, not at all interested in her long-lost offspring. I don't know what made me write like that: perhaps I wanted to keep the dream to myself; perhaps I was growing up; perhaps I wanted to shield myself from something that might well be true.

Anyway, it won that month's prize: ten pounds.

I was torn between two extremes. Happy at having won, at seeing my name in print, at having ten pounds of my own, I wavered between wanting to tell them — to display the pages, the talent, the cheque — and a desire to keep the news entirely to myself. I didn't know how she would react: after all, the story was supposed to be based on fact, and I had used my own name — that is, Katie Gilson. But I couldn't take the chance. So I stayed quiet.

I received all the adulation I wanted from the other girls at school who took the magazine, and to them I spun a yarn that, because of its mystery, helped them to be silent with the family, and added to my own enigma. The trouble was the money. I had a post-office savings-book, and I paid it into that; but I had to be careful not to treat myself to any luxury, and so arouse suspicion. So there the money stayed.

Until, riding home from school in winter darkness, I opened a newspaper someone had left on the seat, and read that Eva Stewart had been found unconscious in her flat, and taken to hospital.

There was a photograph of her in period costume — a still from her latest film — and the report questioned whether she would be well enough to attend its premier a week ahead.

I kept the paper with me when I left the bus. The house was very quiet: unusually so, since Frank was often home before me; and Greg, who had not yet started work, had either his record-player on full volume, or the television. But she alone was home, sitting in the kitchen, slicing apples for a pie.

'Hallo,' I said.

She didn't answer, merely nodded.

'Eva Stewart's in hospital,' I said.

'Who? Oh . . . her. Where are you going?'

'Just up to my room a minute.'

'I suppose you're going to write another letter?'

Something was wrong. I came back.

'What do you mean?'

She wiped her hands on her apron, stood up and went to the dresser. She lifted an envelope from near the bread-board and waved it.

'From Aunt Mary.'

I still couldn't guess what worried her.

'Oh? So — what's the matter?'

'Listen,' she said, and read part of it aloud. ' "*Has Katie written that letter to the Society yet? I told George about it, and he said there aren't many kids these days who'd have the sense to do that.*" ' She looked up. 'Now, what's that all about?'

Knowing her now, knowing what conditions had been like in the house since they'd been married: the adjustments that came too slowly, the extra responsibility of two boys — the elder a noisy slob, the younger being shaped likewise — the husband losing a little of his polish, the vulgarity I had felt before now beginning to show through — knowing all this, I spoke very quietly and slowly, and told her only of the desire to say thanks, and not the original intention. I was becoming skilled in acting this other sweeter person who bore the name Morris. As I talked, so she relaxed. In the end I could see she was moved, and I had the grace to feel furtive and ashamed as she let the crushed pages fall from her hand, came round the table and put her arms around me and kissed me.

'You wormed it out of her, didn't you?' she said.

I returned her smile.

'Yes.'

'Reconciled now, are you? I mean, you've lost this . . . this wanting to see your real mother?'

'I don't think I'll ever lose that,' I said.

'No, of course not.'

'But I'm not worried about it any more. If I can't know, I can't know. And that's all.'

'That's sensible, Katie. I need you more than ever now, don't I?'

'You're not very happy, are you, Mum?'

She dropped her hands and turned away.

'Of course I am. Now.'

The front door slammed, and Greg came into the room.

'What's cooking?' he said. He picked up a coil of apple-peel and chewed it. 'Hi, sis.'

I went upstairs, and from behind the paperbacks in the low, glass-fronted case, took out my savings-book.

On the news on television that evening they mentioned Eva Stewart. They spoke of her old films and of her come-back; showed the front of the hospital, interviewed the Matron who said *as well as could be expected — a recurrence of the old trouble.*

That was Friday.

The next afternoon I left the house after lunch, got a bus to Westminster, went into a post-office — and then looked around for a florist's. It was a chill, grey day, the river the colour of pewter and the sky seeming to ache with the pressure of snow. Never had the funnels of ships and tugs glowed so bright against the off-white of the Festival Hall; or their calls so muffled, as if swathed in wool.

In the shop every light was on, blazing above ferns and tall vases, the yellow hair of the woman who came forward.

'The *most* expensive?' she said, and looked me up and down. 'Depends what you mean by expensive.'

'Ten pounds' worth,' I said, not really wanting to spend that much, but nettled by her patronizing manner. Which had changed when she spoke again.

'Oh, well, yes. I see. For someone or something special, is it? Let me see now.'

Her hands sped like birds over the massed flowers.

'I can offer you carnations. These are quite nice. Then I could make you up a bunch of early Spring flowers: daffs, and so on. Or there's the . . .'

'What are those?' I said, pointing past the bubbling aquarium.

'Well, those *are* expensive. Beautiful, aren't they? Baccara roses. I could make you up a lovely box of those. Are you sure you want to spend that much?'

'Yes. Yes, I'll have those.'

She began to pull the long stems one by one.

'Do you want us to deliver them?'

'No,' I said. 'I'll take them with me. And I'd like a gift-card.'

'There are some in the rack there. If you'd like to choose . . .'

There was one of an old painting: a courtyard with women in long dresses, and running dogs, and a man leaning from an upstairs window. Inside I wrote *To Eva Stewart with love from Katie Gilson. Get well soon. A Fan.* Then I tore it up, chose the same picture, but wrote this time *To Eva with love from Katie. Get well soon.*

While I waited I watched the slow angel-fish gaping above the coloured stones. Then, the long white, red-ribboned box under my arm, I walked to the hospital, feeling, with the prize-money spent, somehow lighter and freer. And excited.

The swing-doors whispered with their rubber tongues, and I was in the entrance-hall. To the left a reception-desk with a woman in a pale-blue uniform, and to the right two men talking. These stopped when I entered and watched me as I walked across the quiet black and white squares — then began again as the woman stood up.

'These are for Miss Stewart.'

She took the box from me.

'Thank you very much.'

I still stood there as she placed them on the table near the wall.

'Was there anything else?'

Cast down, I half turned away. The men stopped talking.

'*Was* there anything else? Did you want to tell me who they're from?'

'There's a card,' I said. 'Inside. They're from me.'

'Oh, are they? Well, thank you from Miss Stewart.'

One of the men came forward. He leaned on the desk and looked at the woman and back to me.

'Pretty big box,' he said.

'Yes.'

'You buy them?'

'Yes.'

He signalled to the other man.

'Look at her,' he said. Then he turned to the

woman. 'Let her hold the box again, Miss. Right. There you are, Pete. Take it. Smile, girly.'

I smiled. Pete focused his camera. A fizz of white, blinding me for an instant.

'We'll have another on the steps just for luck,' he said. 'All human life is here, as they say. You don't mind, Miss?'

She shook her head.

'I don't want any more taken,' I said.

'You can't refuse the Press, girly. Wouldn't you like your picture in the paper?'

'No,' I said. 'My mother might . . .'

I stopped.

He looked closely at me. His tongue pushed against the black hairs of his moustache.

'Your mother might . . . what?'

'What paper are you from?'

He mentioned one we did not take. By now I was enjoying myself. Acting the part.

'All right,' I said.

'Atta girl.'

Back in the entrance-hall again I was about to hand the box over when the reporter said:

'Why don't you let her take it upstairs?'

'Sorry.'

'At least just to the sister. You'd like that, wouldn't you . . . what's your name?'

'Katie. Yes please.'

'I don't know,' said the woman.

'Come on, don't be a spoil-sport,' he said. 'Looks expensive. How much it knock you back, Katie?' I told him and he whistled. 'Really? Well, you can't let her go now, can you? I'll take her up. Okay? Come on.'

'All right,' she said. 'But down again immediately.'

He saluted.

'Yes, ma'am. Come on, Pete.'

Inside the humming lift he rested his back against the dark panelling and considered me.

'Where'd you get the ten pounds from, Katie?'

By now I realized the danger. I didn't want a story written about me — human life or not.

'I'd rather not say,' I said. 'No comment.'

They both laughed.

The sister on the third floor took the box.

'What are they?' she said.

'Baccara roses,' I said.

'Ten pounds' worth already,' said Pete. 'Let her take them in, eh?'

'Certainly not,' she said. Then she relented a little. 'I think she's awake. I'll just show them to her. Wait here.'

We waited. It was very quiet, the noise of the city suppressed.

'Seen any of her films?' said the reporter, unwrapping a peppermint. 'Oh, excuse me. Want one?'

'No thank you. Yes, I've seen them all.'

'Have you now? Mm.'

'You're forgetting me, Tony,' said Pete.

Tony handed him the partly-unwrapped sweet.

'Untouched by human hand,' he said.

Minutes later the sister came back.

'She wants to see you.'

'We're in,' said Tony. 'Ready, Pete?'

'Just the girl,' said the sister. 'She just wants to see the girl.'

I walked almost blindly after her.

5

What I saw first were the other flowers. They were everywhere: on tables, window-ledges, the mantelpiece. Then, in the centre of all these, the bed, my own roses resting across the yellow coverlet — and then her face. Dark eyes, huge in a pale face. Black hair with a band of yellow silk, almost the same shade as the cover: as if she were tied down, lashed and captive to illness. She lifted the roses so that the fingers of her other hand could touch the petals. Alongside the open box the card, in danger of slipping to the floor. I rescued it as I moved closer.

'Hallo, Katie,' she said. 'Come and sit down.'

'I've got your photograph at home,' I said. 'I don't suppose you remember . . . my letter, I mean?'

'Afraid not, Katie. Never mind.'

Her fingers were restless among the petals.

'These are expensive,' she said.

The card clicked in my hand and I held it still.

'I heard you were ill,' I said. 'It was on the television, too.'

'Did you choose these yourself?'

'Yes.'

'And the money? Or is that a rude question?'

The sister fussed about the room.

'I'll ring when Katie's ready to leave. Thank you.'

She went out and we both heard the men's questioning voices.

'Did you bring some friends?' she said.

'They're reporters.'

She turned her head to the window.

'I thought they'd all gone,' she said. 'Never be an actress, Katie. Your life's not your own.' She looked back at me. 'I was asking you about the money.'

'You've got plenty of others. If I had known I would have brought you something different.'

'Yours are the nicest of all,' she said. 'Before you go we'll put them in water, and they can have pride of place. Can you put them over there for a moment?'

Free of them, she straightened the coverlet and the sheets, and I helped rearrange her pillows. She sank back with a sigh.

'Now — the money,' she said.

And I told her about the story in *Beatrice*, the news of her illness, the florists. And then back to the beginning — the photograph in *The People*, the resemblance: this last mentioned with some hesitancy, but with an undercurrent of pride.

'Still think you look like me?' she said. 'Or vice-versa?'

'I . . . I don't know,' I said.

She picked up a small ivory-handled mirror and looked at herself. And winced.

'You don't look as tired,' she said. '. . . and after that?'

The letter, the photograph. Signed.

'Stamped,' she said. 'You know why. I'd like to . . . but it's impossible.'

The door opened and the sister leaned in.

'Not *too* long please, Miss Stewart.'

'Bring a vase will you, please? For these.'

'If I can find another,' she said. The door rustled her stiff uniform.

'Have you seen any of my films, Katie?'

'No,' I said. 'You see . . .'

'Don't apologize.'

'No, we lived in a village, you see, and I didn't go to the pictures much.'

'Where was that?'

I could see she was beginning to become weary, but I launched into my life-story — interrupted by the entry of the vase.

She showed me where to cut the stems and how to mash the ends, and when they were all upright we placed them on the trolley near her bed. During all this the sister stayed in the room, and once the job was done, pounced.

'I think that's enough, Miss Stewart.'

'Have you read *Lorna Doone,* Katie? The film I've just made?'

'Yes. A long time ago. I've got it at home somewhere.'

'That's a pity,' she said. 'I was going to get you a copy so that you could have it next time you come.'

Next time you come.

'I wouldn't mind reading it again.'

'Isn't there something else?' she said. 'I must give you something for these beautiful flowers. All your prize money. Haven't you a favourite author, or something?'

'There's Richard O'Dell,' I said. 'I've read nearly all of his.'

'I don't know him,' she said. 'Hand Katie that pad, will you, Sister? And the pen. You write down there what you've read of his — and I'll get you one you haven't. If I can.'

'You don't have to,' I said, busy writing. When I had finished she took the paper and studied it.

'Now, today's Saturday. Would you like to come on Monday, just for a minute or so?'

And it was arranged.

'Give me a kiss before you go,' she said, and I leaned forward, into smoothness and perfume.

At the end of the corridor the two men straightened and followed me into the lift.

'Well, how is she?' said Pete.

'Better than I thought she'd be,' I said. 'What's wrong with her, do you know?'

'Heart, isn't it?' said Pete.

'Heart,' said Tony. 'What did you talk about?'

'Oh, her films — everything.'

'Where do you live, Katie?'

'I told you — no comment.'

'She tell you to say that?' said Pete.

'No comment.'

'You coming to see her again?'

'On Monday,' I said. 'You can have that.'

The next day I managed to look through most of the Sunday papers. But there were no reports or photographs, and I was more pleased than sorry. I was getting tired of a life of intrigue and cover-up.

The day passed slowly enough with the ritual of Sunday dinner and the somnolent afternoon spent reading or watching old films on television while snow stung the windows. I had been invited out to tea by a girl from school and, about four, began to get ready.

'Take Katie to her friend's, Jack,' she said.

'Eh?' he said, looking up from his cards.

'Oh, no,' said Greg. 'Not now. Not till I get my half-a-crown back.'

'Look at the weather,' she said. 'It's not far, Jack. Just over Putney Bridge.'

'It doesn't matter,' I said, aware of his irritation. 'I

don't mind snow. I go by bus every day.'

'Course you do,' he said. 'Not coming down that much.' He looked at his cards. 'I'll go a risky bundle.'

'You would,' said Greg. 'We know your risky bundles. I pass. Can't you stop him, Frank?'

'Nothing here,' said Frank. 'Look who dealt.'

'*Jack*,' she said. 'Please.'

'Mum, it doesn't matter.'

'If she says it doesn't matter, leave it, Alice.'

I was glad to get out into the clean cold air.

Monday, too, crawled. But at last I was home and getting changed out of that stupid school uniform.

'Where did you say you were going?' she said, when I came down and entered the kitchen.

'Oh, just up West with Sally,' I said. 'Can I have a sandwich or something? I don't want to wait for the others.'

'They won't be in, either. Jack's gone up to Manchester — he phoned this afternoon. Greg's gone with him. And Frank's with someone else. I've got a nice piece of fish here, too.'

'Not for me, Mum. Just a sandwich.'

'You can wait.'

'I can't, Mum. I'm meeting Sally at six.'

'You've got plenty of time.'

'I haven't, Mum. We've got to be there early.'

'Where?'

'. . . there's some Sale on. Sally wants me to help her choose something.'

'I thought I was going to have a family,' she said. 'Cheese do? Or salmon?'

'Cheese.'

I didn't have to be there until six-thirty, but lately the house had become oppressive, and I couldn't just relax as I used to at the flat. I wanted to be out, and had planned to walk around the shops or at least have a cup of coffee while I waited.

'You watch yourself up there, Katie,' she said. 'You look older than you are.'

'I won't be that long,' I said. 'I'll be back by eight.'

'You'd better be,' she said. 'Or I'll have something to say to Sally.'

Once out of the house I felt myself again — free of Jack and his sons, free of a mother who was not my own; the streets full of light and movement, busy with another life, a life I wanted to be part of.

I was at the hospital five minutes before time. The receptionist looked up from her desk. It was a different woman.

'Is it all right for me to go up?' I said, almost without stopping. 'I know the way. Miss Stewart's.'

'You just wait a moment. Is your name Katie?'

I paused near the lift, and went back.

'Yes.'

'Then this is for you,' she said, and, reaching

down under the counter, she handed me a square brown package.

'Can't I go up?' I said.

'There's a letter inside,' she said.

I went across the hall and sat on the blue leather of the long seat. Tucked inside a copy of Richard O'Dell's *Godseye* was a folded slip of white paper. Small slanting hand.

My dear Katie,

I've been told I'm not to have any more visitors for a while. I'm sorry. Here's the book I promised you. It looks interesting. Perhaps we can meet again soon. Thank you for the roses: still the best.

Love,
Eva Stewart

I carefully re-wrapped the book, and crossed to the desk.

'Could I phone her from here? Just to speak for a minute?'

'Sorry,' she said. 'She's resting, and most probably asleep. You can write a note if you like. Here.'

I took the pen and rested the pad on the counter. I had just started writing when the phone rang near my hand. She picked it up and listened for a moment.

'Yes,' she said. 'I'll do that right away. Thank you.'

She replaced the receiver and reached over and put her hand over mine.

'I don't think that will be necessary now, dear. I'm afraid that what we thought might happen, has. Miss Stewart died a little while ago. I'm sorry. Now, I have a lot of calls to make. If you want to stay, you . . .'

'No,' I said, screwing up the paper. 'I'll go.'

She began dialling as I walked away.

I can't remember much of what I did for the next hour or so of that evening. I can recall a blur of traffic, of shop-windows, of noise and of trees dripping melted snow around street-lamps. I must have walked miles, the book clutched to me, my eyes on nothing, my feet going their own way and the rest of my body following. I was more stunned than unhappy. I felt an ache as when a nerve is pressed and then released: a bruising aftermath.

But I pulled myself together as, walking near a church, I heard its clock strike half-past seven. I caught a bus, and went home.

'I was beginning to wonder,' she said.

'I'm only ten minutes late,' I said. And suddenly I was ravenously hungry.

'I suppose I can do you the fish,' she said. 'Frank phoned to say he's had his out, and I've only had a snack.'

'Eva Stewart's dead.'

'You been crying?'

'No.'

'A shame,' she said. 'How did you hear?'

'It's . . . it's in the papers.'

'Not in ours,' she said. 'Must be a late edition.'

'Stop press,' I said. 'I'll be down in a minute and help.'

And I went upstairs. Before I put the book away I looked again at the dedication: *To Katie — the girl with the roses — from Eva Stewart*. Then I slid the glass doors shut.

After we had eaten, it was time for the news on television. He began to speak, and behind him her face appeared.

'That's the picture you've got upstairs,' she said. 'Only thirty. What a shame. I was only thinking the other day the number of people who . . .'

But I was remembering a room full of flowers, a yellow hair-band, and entering smoothness and perfume.

As if instinctively: a sinking of myself in something she had touched, which was both mine and hers — perhaps even to rid myself of her memory — I began that night to read *Godseye*. It was difficult at first: I kept putting down the book and closing my eyes. The rest of the house silent, asleep. The small excited tick of the alarm, the odd gearchange heard in the street below, emphasizing the quiet.

But before sleep came, once again the story held me. And I dreamed that night of the Inca temples, the sacrificial dawn, the high-priests and the young warriors; and in between the strange processions and the dancers the face of Eva Stewart weaved, and spoke words forgotten on waking.

It was announced in the paper that the funeral was to be on Thursday, at Liphook, her home town in Hampshire. I decided I would go. This meant missing school, and I thought of pretending to be ill in the morning, and to be better by lunchtime. But in the end I decided to go out of the house as usual, and to catch a train from Waterloo at about ten. This would give me time to get some flowers (I had over three pounds in my savings-book from earlier deposits), and to walk around until the service.

I was lucky that the sun shone that morning: a pale shadow of its summer self, not warming, but at least present. I don't think I could have borne rain. I caught the train as planned (not for a minute did I consider the excuse I would have to give the following day), and by eleven I had arrived in Liphook. After a hot pie and a cup of tea in the transport café outside the station I sat in the local park for a while, bundled-up against the day, the flowers beside me, and read O'Dell's book. The weather was somehow different from any other day. It was probably me that was different — emotional at the coming ceremony; elated and suspended by the story I was reading; guilty at my first truancy, thinking of the others working — but I will always remember the *shifting* quality of cloud and sunlight: swathes of light chased by bands and blocks of darkness, covering me one by one. I remember the white dog that sniffed around my shoes until its owner called it away; the kite that spun over and over in the air, its tail cracking like a whip; a boy going by with a fishing-rod and an empty jar.

The cemetery was on the other side of the park: I had asked a gardener digging the hard earth. As I neared the lych-gate a sudden shower came, and I stood under the shelter until it passed. The sun was brilliant by comparison with the dark scudding clouds. A rainbow arched overhead and a blackbird sang.

There were many cars and many mourners. No one took any notice of me, and when the service began I sat at the back near black radiator-pipes that gave off a hot, somehow breathless smell. One of the hymns was one we often had at school, but I did not join in.

Then the long walk to where the hole was waiting. This was what I had been dreading, but such was the sunlight that the scene seemed oddly festive with the blackbird still singing, and the blue sky and the hundreds of flowers. I joined the procession, again at the rear. I recognized a few famous stars. They seemed ordinary, unexceptional. Not as she had been. We walked through avenues of many old graves, and the raindrops from the shower winked on open books made of marble, the fixed stone feathers of doves, the rinsed dust-trailed faces of angels and cherubs.

The words were said. I noticed a wagtail bouncing near a puddle. A woman sniffed and a man coughed. The earth spattered the shiny wood. It was over. So quickly.

One by one they moved away, talking softly, seemingly relieved. I waited until they were all gone, off in the direction of the church and main road; then I moved closer and laid my flowers on the edge with the others. I can never explain what made me do and say the stupid things I did in the next ten minutes.

I stood by the open hole, looking down. It was the first and only time I have ever been to a funeral, and I suppose that standing there alone it was natural that I should think of my father. It could be him down there and not Eva Stewart. What was amazing was the beauty of the day. In the pale grass near the hole the rain sparkled like tiny globes of coloured glass. The blackbird sang its heart out — and both my father and Eva were dead.

I turned away suddenly — and ran straight into the hard body of a man. I looked up.

'Well, well, look who's here,' said Tony.

Behind him stood Pete, camera at the ready.

'Take it easy,' said Tony. 'What's the rush?'

I moved to get past, but he held me.

'On your own?' he said.

'Yes. Please can I go?'

'I hear you were at the hospital again on Monday,' he said.

'I told you I would be,' I said. 'Let go.'

'What's the attraction?' he said. 'Look, Pete, look at her face. Are you a relation?'

'Please let me go.'

'You can go, dear. Just tell me your name.'

'Katie Gilson.'

'And what school is this?' he said, touching the badge on my hat.

I wrenched free, slipped on the wet grass, and landed on a pile of damp earth.

'Oops,' he said, helping me up. '*Are* you a relation? Or just one of the fan-club?'

'No, I'm not one of her fans,' I said flustered, dashing pieces of soil from my hands, the book loose under my arm. 'I think she might be my mother.'

'Wow!' said Pete, and lifted his camera.

'Your mother?' said Tony. 'What did I tell you, Pete boy?'

Pete took another picture.

'Do you mean that?' said Tony. 'Eva Stewart was your mother?'

'I look like her, don't I?'

'Yes.'

'And I'm adopted.'

'Look, Katie,' he said. 'What say we . . .'

But I saw my opportunity, and I ran. Ran as fast as I could go, saying to myself at each jolting step over stone and grass, *my mother, my mother*. Behind me they called again and again. But I did not stop until I was out of the churchyard and into the park.

Could she have been my mother? She could. She could easily have had me when she was under twenty: eighteen, seventeen. Easily.

I sat in the train and rubbed my fingers over the brown spots on the cover of my book, and then began to read. When we pulled into Waterloo I had only a few pages left; and I actually finished it during the last stage of the bus journey, closing it as we stopped.

Luckily no one had called to ask why I had not been at school. She had just gone upstairs to tell Greg to turn down his record-player; Frank was using one of her best dusters to clean the mud off his football-boots — and the kettle was whistling furiously in the kitchen — so in the noise and the complaining and the confusion I managed to scoot upstairs, sponge some of the earth-marks from my skirt and my sleeve, and change into jeans and a sweater before any questions could be asked.

But there were questions to be asked later. And how.

Tea was ready, in fact long-ready and overdue (we were all waiting for Jack to come home) — when the front-door bell sounded.

'Forgotten his key again,' said Greg.

'Well, go and let him in,' she said.

'Let Frank go,' he said. 'I'm watching this.'

'Get the casserole out of the oven, Katie,' she said. 'I'll let him in.'

'Good,' said Frank, putting down his magazine. 'I'm starved.'

I got a raffia-mat from the drawer and started to transfer the casserole to the table. She entered the kitchen — and behind her were Tony and Pete.

6

You can imagine what they had done, Miss Roberts. One had driven the car back to London, and the other had followed me across the park, on to the station and the train — and home. I had noticed nothing, possibly because I was deep in the book. Then they had joined-up again, and called at the house.

You can imagine, too, what was said while they were there — and what was said *after* they had gone.

She was upset: the old wound had opened again, and her daughter — her adopted daughter — still rejected her in favour of a dream-mother. And what was harder to bear, had used deceit and lies, had spent more money on a dead film-star than ever she had spent on the woman who had loved and cared for her over the years. Ungrateful, selfish . . . the hard words multiplied. Added to this the truancy, the possible report in a national paper which would discredit both herself and Eva Stewart: a holiday for gossip; the pointing fingers, the whispers. All because of a girl who lived more in a dream-world than in the reality of a good step-father, a house, a good school, adequate pocket-money. Etcetera, etcetera. Which, of course, was all true. For her.

Jack, coming home half-way in the scene, took a while to realize what was happening — but, when he did, used the same sort of humour as Greg and Frank — more tolerant perhaps, since there was an edge to the boys' snorts and chuckles which spoke of cruelty, or at least, incomprehension.

The reporters were disappointed. After a while they went away, promising not even to use the story of one fan who stayed away from school in order to attend her favourite's funeral. It was all in the game: win one, lose another.

As for me, I felt detached from all the recriminations, the worried, questioning look on her face; the boys' snide comments. I felt sorry for her, but I knew that this was the beginning of the end for us. What possibility there had been for a closer life together: the grateful daughter saying *Thank you, thank you* or *I love you Mum* — this seemed to shrivel by the hour. I was glad it was all out in the open. I don't like a bad conscience. I knew also that I had treated her badly, that I could be kinder from now on. But something in me, perhaps which was truly me, a part of my own undiscovered heredity, was unrelenting; and life between us — between all of us — from that evening on, became a matter of artificial politeness, of doing and saying only what was necessary. And, for me, a growing more apart, a using of the house as merely a place to sleep in, have meals, endure until I was old enough to live what I began to call my own share of the world.

I was almost thirteen then, and the years to sixteen were surprisingly uneventful. I lived inside myself, had a few friends, was aware of my budding body, had crushes on various boys which came to nothing other than a misjudged kiss as I kept one eye on the film.

My relations with my adopted mother were those of monks or nuns with their superiors — except that they accepted, however unwilling at times, the discipline of obedience — and I did not. I merely waited for the years to roll by — and, living as I did within myself, it was not too difficult. Greg had decided not to enter his father's business, and had chosen catering instead. He now worked at a hotel in Devon. Frank left school as soon as he was able, and became a mechanic in a garage. I saw little of him. Her relations with Jack were amiable, if not anything wildly romantic. They accepted, I think, that they had chosen unwisely — but neither had the energy to do anything about it. For him, life was the business, the buying of new cars, drinks with his customers and associates, and home weary to a meal, to TV and bed. She, now that she felt my ingratitude, worked as a doctor's receptionist; joined a number of societies devoted to the elderly; tried two or three times to spark some regard, some warmth, between us, then gave up.

As my sixteenth birthday drew near, they asked me what I would like as a present. I said a bicycle; but that morning I discovered he had bought me a motor-scooter. It stood in the hall, its red enamel gleaming, its chromium reflecting the coat-rack and the glass panels of the front door.

'Better than a bike,' he said. 'Easy as pie to ride. One day I'll teach you to drive a car, Katie. But this'll do until then. Give you a chance to get used to the road.'

Perhaps trying to buy my love (no, that is unfair — they did it out of kindness), they did not realize that they had unwittingly given me the means of widening the gap still further. For that summer I went all over the place, at first on my own, taking a book and landing-up in some field or other, or on the fringe of cliffs; then, when Pat Saunders bought one secondhand, we would go together, sleeping-bags strapped to the back, every southern county open to us.

One Sunday, sitting on a farm-gate, eating our sandwiches and drinking hot coffee from the flask, the summer holidays approaching, I said:

'What about taking off for France this August?

We could get by with the language — you better than me.'

She pursed her lips. Then shook her head.

'I don't think they'd let me, Katie. *She* might, but he wouldn't. Remember the fuss he kicked up the first time we wanted to sleep out? I don't think yours would, either, would she?'

'She might — if you got permission.'

She shook her head again.

'I don't think he . . .'

'Well, just suggest it. See what they say. Hundreds do it, Pat.'

It had a surprising outcome. They wouldn't let Pat go — but offered instead to take us both with them to France — if France was what we wanted. It *was* what I wanted — but I couldn't stand her parents.

(As I write this, Miss Roberts, I feel somehow that I ought to say otherwise — give another, pleasanter portrait of myself. But I can only write down what is true. If I begin to feel I *have* been selfish — perhaps I have. But who isn't?)

No, I have to be truthful. I *did* dislike her parents. They were the museum, art-gallery, organized-tour sort of people. And somehow I, who might have liked that sort of holiday earlier, now wanted something more. And I wanted to be free of adults, not anchored to them for two weeks.

So in the end Pat went with them, and I faced the prospect of going with my adopted mother to, as usual, one of the south coast resorts — where Jack would sleep under a newspaper in his deckchair, and she would comment on the skimpiness of bikinis.

But it turned out very differently.

I'll have to go back a few months. There had been a long silence from Richard O'Dell since he had published *Godseye*. I kept a look-out in reviews of new novels, but his name was always absent. I re-read his others often, and one afternoon at school, in a library free-period, I wrote a letter to him, care of the publishers, asking if and when a new book was due.

About a week later I received this reply.

Dear Miss Gilson,

I have a new novel coming out in July. It is called The Apprentice.

Thank you for all you say about

Richard O'Dell

The address was a place I had not heard of before: just outside Winchester. I wrote again, saying how glad I was, and that I was looking forward to reading it. To this I received no reply.

I asked the local library to reserve me a copy, and one morning, just as I was going upstairs after breakfast, I saw the card fall to the mat.

'Is it for me?' she called.

'No. It's from the library. A book I wanted is in.'

I collected it on the way home from school.

Once again it had a marvellous cover (all his books are designed by the same artist). It showed a panoramic view of London in the seventeenth century: the spires, the bridges over the silver river, the fields at the edges of the city. Inside, the blurb outlined the story of a weaver's apprentice caught up in the Great Plague.

It was a shorter book than his others, but again very readable, and by the time I had finished it I felt I had actually lived through all the fortunes of Thomas Fairfax. Although the pages were new, they seemed to breathe the same aged smell as I had known in the old book I had found in Soho. It took some time to return to normal.

As soon as I could I wrote to him. Back came a short note of thanks. No encouragement to proceed further. But now I had the scooter I thought of going down to see him. I was interested in that lean face which always looked out from the back of his books. But his next letter said *I shall be out of the country until the end of July. Perhaps another time.*

Now it was the middle of August. Pat was in France with her parents, and we were due for Bournemouth in two weeks' time.

On Thursday I joined her for the usual lunch at the café after she had worked that morning at the surgery.

'Do you mind very much if I don't come this time?'

'Of course I do,' she said. 'What would you do with yourself?'

'Oh, I could find plenty . . .'

'You should have gone with that school trip to Greece. You wouldn't be so bored now. You know Jack was agreeable. And it *was* a lot of money.'

'He could afford it.'

'That's not the point. You would have been enjoying yourself now instead . . .'

'I get enough of teachers and kids,' I said. 'Can I? Not come, I mean?'

'I'm not leaving you in London on your own,' she said. 'You should have thought of all this before. Why you didn't go with Pat, I don't know. They're nice people. I bet she's having a wonderful time. Other children would be glad of . . .'

'I'm not other children,' I said. '*Please*. I can find enough to do.'

'No. You should have arranged something before this. Stayed with a friend, or something.'

'Perhaps it's not too late. I could still fix something up. There's Charlotte — she's not gone away, and . . .'

'The hotel's been booked for the three of us. I'm sorry, Katie, but you'll have to come. We'll have trips every day, and I know that Jack and I need a break, even if you don't.'

7

But what I did get out of them was permission for me to ride down to Bournemouth on my scooter, and not go with them in one of his cars. I thought that as long as I had it with me down there, at least I would have the means of escape if I wanted to.

The evening before we were due to go I was sitting in the living-room checking my route on the map, when I saw that, if I liked, I could go by way of Winchester, and so could call on Richard O'Dell. After all, he was home now from whatever part of the world he had been — and he *had* said *Perhaps another time*.

I said nothing to them about my decision — just mentioned that they were not to expect me until around tea-time.

And the next day I strapped my case on to the grid at the back, waved goodbye to them standing on the steps, and roared off.

I thoroughly enjoyed the ride down. Pleasant day, the wind whipping past me, the country opening up its freedom. I was in Winchester by just after twelve, found the small hamlet where he lived; then the lane, and then the house.

It was a disappointment. I had envisaged something much larger, bearing sophistication; by its setting and its look declaring that here lived a creative person, an artist, a shaper of minds. But it was just a bungalow, detached among a row of equally insignificant houses: all the same type, each with its neatly clipped hedge, its bird-table, its car-port. Only, his hedge was untidy, the bird-table leaned, and the grass of the front garden was long and starred with daisies. Now that I was there, the noise of the engine spluttering to silence, I had sudden second thoughts. But I had made the journey — I was there. Best to go through with it. He could always slam the door in my face — but at least I would have seen him.

I loosed the straps on the case and opened it. I took out my copy of *Godseye*, restrapped the case, and leaving my crash-helmet on the seat, walked over to the gate. It was a very quiet lane, and as I paused at the door of the house I could hear bees busy among the flowers under the left-hand window.

I rang the bell.

Immediately there was the high yapping of a dog somewhere in the interior, a skittering of paws on tiles or linoleum, a succession of sharp excited breaths under the door and a few more barks. Then a door opened and closed inside, and a voice said:

'That's enough, Marcus. Be quiet.'

The dog stopped barking, the catch was slipped, and I looked into the face of a small grey-haired woman with bright blue eyes behind rimless spectacles. She was dressed in a thick woollen cardigan over a check blouse, a green skirt and scruffy-looking bedroom-slippers whose age was evident in their pale much-worn ochre colour. A small white terrier was trapped by her right leg. It struggled, and then was quiet, its tongue trembling.

'Is this Richard O'Dell's house?' I said.

'Yes.'

'I wonder if I could see him? Just for a moment?'

'I'm afraid he's abroad.'

'I thought he said he'd be back by July.'

'How do you know that?'

'I've got a letter from him.'

'Oh? Have you got it with you?'

'Yes.'

I took the book from under my arm, opened it and handed her the sheet.

'So you're Katie Gilson, are you?'

'Has he mentioned me?'

'Oh, I know your name. But he's still abroad, I'm afraid.'

'I've come all the way from London,' I said. 'I *did* want to see him.'

'I see you've got *Godseye* there.'

'Yes. I wanted him to sign it for me.'

'Well, if you leave it with me I'll get him to do it when he returns.'

'When will that be?'

'Any day now. I'll post it to you, don't worry.'

'Well, I'm on my way down to Bournemouth, you see. I could always call in if I knew he was back. Shall I take his phone-number and ring every day? Just to see?'

'You must want to meet him very much.'

'I do. I think he's a marvellous writer. I want to be a writer myself, and I thought . . .'

'Do you now? Be quiet, Marcus.'

'Are you his . . .' I didn't know how to guess the relationship. '. . . his wife?'

She laughed.

'No, no. Just his housekeeper.' She looked at me for a few seconds. 'Well, as you've come especially out of your way, you had better come in.'

Marcus padded ahead of us into the living-room. It was simply furnished: table, chairs, bookcases; watercolours of fruit and flowers. Rich-looking carpet. A large radiogram with a record in place, but not playing.

'Taken it all in?' she said.

'I'm sorry,' I said. 'I didn't mean to . . .'

'Don't you be sorry,' she said. 'That's what a writer has got to do: snap, snap, with the camera.

Richard's always saying that. Sharpen the eye — so that by closing it you can remember everything. Close your eyes.'

'Pardon?'

'Go on, close your eyes. We'll see if you can make a writer. That's it. Now, what's wrong with my dog?'

'He limps.'

'Right. What foot?'

'Front left.'

'Good. What's the reason?'

I opened my eyes.

'I don't know, do I?'

'You're a writer. Why does he limp?'

'Er . . . caught in a trap.'

'Wrong. But it'll do. Boxer had a go at him. Shut your eyes again. What is the picture above the fireplace?'

'Er . . . Venice?'

'Good.'

'Water-colour.'

'Yes. By whom?'

'I don't know.'

'I expect too much,' she said. 'Now, don't open them yet. Describe me.'

And I did.

'Excellent. Only I'm not all grey, my dear. Still got some brown in there, somewhere. What's the newest thing in the room?'

'The carpet?'

'Wrong. You can open them now. Now what?'

'The radiogram?'

'Right. Do you like Debussy?'

'Yes.'

'Listen,' she said. The soft music washed around the room like a slowly rolling invisible sea.

'Doesn't he mind you playing his records?'

'How do you know they're his?'

'I'm sorry. I thought . . .'

She laughed.

'No, he doesn't mind. Very tolerant, is Richard. Now, what would you like? Tea, coffee, milk, orange, fruit-juice. Even a sherry.'

'No thank you. I think . . .'

'Ever had a sherry?'

'Yes.'

'Describe its taste.'

'Oh, thick, brown, sweet . . .'

'Then you'll have a dry,' she said. 'A Manzanilla. You'll have to distinguish if you're going to be a writer. Oh, but wait a minute. You came by bike, didn't you?'

'Scooter.'

'I don't want you having any accidents.'

'I'd rather have coffee anyway.'

'So would I,' she said. 'It's a good thing Richard isn't here — you'd be the gentleman from Porlock all over again. Do you know about that?'

'Yes. Coleridge. *Kubla Khan*.'

She stopped outside a door and looked back.

'So they do teach you something in those schools.'

'I read it myself, I think.'

'Of course,' she said. 'Who ever learned anything at school?'

I helped her butter the bread and make the cucumber sandwiches. Marcus whined around and was given a biscuit.

'Where does he write?' she said. 'In the back room. I'll show it to you later.'

'Have you been his housekeeper long?'

'Years,' she said. 'A long time.'

'He never married?'

'No. He likes being alone.'

'Where is he now?'

'Don't you ask a lot of questions?'

'A writer has to.'

She laughed again and nodded.

'*Touché*. I'll tell you later. Now, let me ask you about yourself.'

And while we ate the sandwiches and drank the coffee and listened to another record, and Marcus snored in a patch of sunlight, I told her everything. She was a very good listener, rarely interrupting — yet, if she did, seeming to help the flow rather than impede it.

'And so you never have found your real mother?'

'No.'

'Sad. But good in a way, don't you think?'

'Good? How?'

'Think of all the mothers you *can* have. In a way you're very lucky. Most of us have only one mother. You can have as many as you like. Duchesses, gipsies, princesses, housewives in Manchester, Wigan or ... Venice. All the women in the world. You can have a new one every day. Can't you?'

'That's one way of looking at it.'

'There's always more than one way of looking at *anything*,' she said. 'Thank God.'

The record finished, the arm clicked back into silence.

'Do you want anything more to eat?' she said. 'I could make more sandwiches.'

'No thank you,' I said. 'Let me help wash up.'

'We'll leave it for now,' she said. 'I'll do it later. If you want to see where he works ...'

I stood up and followed her out of the room and along the hall to a room to the left. Sunlight streamed in, warming the ranks of books which filled three walls. Again simply furnished: a large table with an antiquated Underwood, two chairs, a low divan. French windows showed a corner of the garden — the grass here also overgrown, half-covering a small rusty roller.

She stood beside me.

'I know it ought to look neater, but I don't like

everything straightened out and tidy. Besides, it's an endless job — cut it, and you're doing it every week or so. I just wait until I can't see the next house, then I have one big desperate day — and that lasts for another six months.'

'Has he read all these?' I said, going from shelf to shelf.

'At one time or another. Can't throw anything away.'

'Ah,' I said, as I discovered his own titles. 'Which one do you like best?'

'I haven't read any.'

I swung round, amazed.

'You haven't? With him in the same house! Why, if I lived in the same house I'd . . .'

'What would you do?'

'Well, I wouldn't be able to wait until the next one came out. I'd be reading it over his shoulder as he typed.'

She smiled.

'I was only joking. I've read them all, of course. Which one do you like?'

'I've read them all, too,' I said. 'Except this one.' I showed her the copy of *Evaline* I had taken from the shelf. 'I don't seem to be able to get it.'

'It's been out of print for a long time,' she said. 'That's the only copy left.'

'It was his first, then?'

'Yes. Not very good. A beginning. You were telling me which one you liked the . . .'

'I think *Boy Pan,*' I said. 'Although I've enjoyed them all.'

'Yes,' she said. 'I've a fondness for that. Of course, all the critics said it was *devoid of the logic that fantasy must possess* — or something.'

I looked around, *Evaline* still in my hand.

'It's a nice room,' I said.

'Come back into the living-room,' she said. 'And bring that with you.'

Marcus pushed himself off the rug and followed us.

Once back in the room she exchanged her glasses for another pair and found a pen from the sideboard.

'Where's your *Godseye?*' she said.

I handed it to her.

'What are you going to do?' I said.

She sat down at the table.

'This will be worth a lot of money one day,' she said, smiling. 'A film-star's signature — and now the author's.'

'You can't write his . . .'

Her smile broadened and she began to write.

'Haven't you guessed yet?' she said.

And she passed it back to me. *Richard O'Dell*. The same signature as in the letters.

'You're . . .'

'Yes,' she said, her glasses now in her hands. 'I'm Richard O'Dell.'

'But the photograph on all your books . . .'

'Oh, part of an innocent deception,' she said. 'Actually, it's my brother.'

'Doesn't he mind?'

'Oh, he thoroughly enjoys the thought of being an absent author,' she said. 'He lives in Italy. In Florence.'

'But what is your real name?'

'It *is* O'Dell,' she said. 'Georgina. Isn't that terrible? It's not me at all. You see, when I first began writing seriously: you know, the first stumbling efforts — poems and short stories — I used to use my own name. Then I began to dislike the patronizing way women-writers were discussed and considered — also I wanted to tackle different subjects; and when I had written my first novel under my own name, and it had been returned again and again, I decided to rewrite it and send it out under the flag of *Richard* O'Dell. They took it right away, and I saw it as a sign of good luck. Also it preserves my anonymity — not that I'm terribly well known — but I like my privacy. That's why he's always out if anyone calls — and his housekeeper apologizes.'

'Why tell me, then?'

'I don't know,' she said. 'Well, of course I do, really. I like you. Feel you're sincere. And I'm in-between books at present. If I *had* been working, Marcus would have seen you off! And it's nice to talk to someone who *has* read my books — and not going to one day. Disappointed? Did you expect some handsome artistic type?'

'Yes,' I said. 'But not disappointed.'

'And I'm going to do you a great favour, Katie. You can borrow *Evaline*. But please take care of it. It's the only copy left in the world, so far as I can see. Send it back to me when you've finished it.'

'I will,' I said. 'I'll take care of it.'

'Are you writing anything yourself at the moment?'

'No.'

'Well, you ought to be getting into practice,' she said.

'Would you read it if I sent it to you?'

'If it's not too long,' she said. 'I've got my own living to get, too.'

'A short story?'

'Anything you like.'

'Something that really happened?'

'The old advice is *write what you know*. But it's not always so. Sometimes you can know something in your imagination better than something outside it.'

'Like the Incas in *Godseye*.'

'Yes,' she said. 'I would have made a wonderful high-priestess in another incarnation.'

And as we looked at each other I felt that here was someone who really understood me: that beneath the thick cardigan was a person who had enough breadth of mind to be both father and mother, brother and sister — everyone.

'I'd better go now,' I said.

She came with me to the door, and down the path to the gate. Once again I marvelled that this commonplace, ordinary-looking woman could house such landscapes as a sick seventeenth-century city, Inca temples and the animal-haunted mind of a boy.

'Don't forget,' she said, as I put both books into the case, 'take care of *Evaline*. And don't be too long sending it back.'

'I won't,' I said. 'And I will send you a story, soon.'

'Yes,' she said. 'And keep my secret.'

'Mr. O'Dell is still out of the country.'

'That's right. In foreign parts. The more foreign the better.'

She stayed by the gate, waving, until I turned into the road, and the wall of a house hid her from view.

I had ridden along the main Bournemouth road for about ten minutes, when I swung into a lay-by and stopped the engine.

The thought of staying at the hotel for two weeks

completely depressed me. During the visit I had felt keenly alive — as if I belonged in the same world as that mind-travelling woman; as if I had only to take pen and paper to enter it, and be her companion. Her interest had inspired me — for good or ill — and I felt I had to get her opinion on something of my own.

Cars and motor-bikes flashed by, heading for the coast.

But not me. I started the engine again, swung round in the direction of London, and rode until I saw a telephone-box. I got the number of the hotel from directory-inquiries (there was no book on the ledge), and rang through.

'Could I speak to Mrs. Morris, please?' (It still sounded strange: *Morris*.) 'Or Mr? They arrived today.'

Slight pause.

'Mr. and Mrs. Morris have not arrived yet. Can I take a message?'

They had probably stopped on the way for a meal. And I was glad. Sweat dripped from my face, and not merely because of the sun beating on red metal and glass panels.

'Yes, please. This is their daughter, Katie. I'm supposed to be staying at the hotel with them.'

'That's correct.'

'Well, I'm sorry, but could you tell them something has come up and I won't be coming? Tell them not to worry, I'll be staying at home. I'll ring them this evening.'

'You will not be coming at all?'

'No.'

'But the reservation . . .?'

'Tell them if there's any trouble, I'll pay it back.'

'Very well.'

The air was cool and beautiful as I opened the door.

During the ride home my mind was half on what I was going to write. I didn't want to touch the adoption bit. I felt clear of that for the first time in years. I had my own life to live, hadn't I? What if I were adopted? It could have been a lot worse. I was my own girl — and beginning to be proud of it.

Because we were going to be away for two weeks, Frank had arranged to stay with friends. So the house was mine for all that long beautiful time.

I hadn't much money for food — in fact I hadn't thought of food at all — but, once near home, I bought some eggs and sausages, and made a meal in the kitchen, with the transistor tinkling beside the plate.

I washed-up and went to my room. I took out an old exercise-book, placed *Godseye* and *Evaline* on the window-ledge in front of me, filled my pen and sat down.

But it wasn't that easy. After a long time,

crouched over the table, with the evening darkening to night, all I had to show was a waste-bin full of a dozen different beginnings.

I put the pen down, crumpled the page I had been working on, and stretched my arms above my head. Then I decided I had better phone them in Bournemouth — perhaps this was nagging at the back of my mind, and I couldn't settle until it was done. But once the operator had said *Number please*, my courage failed me and I couldn't answer. Back in my room again, at the table, my restlessness increased — and in the end I decided to go out for a walk. I'd phone from a box somewhere. I picked up *Evaline* — I don't know why, perhaps as a talisman, or with some idea of beginning it while I was out — and left the house.

It was a warm evening, and once outside in the streets I felt better. I walked slowly; until, night come truly now, I turned from Earls Court Road and into Kensington High Street. Crossing near the Odeon I heard the music; and when I had reached the other side, I stopped and looked at the procession marching towards me.

8

Leading it were a group of musicians — two guitars, a banjo, a trumpet and a trombone. They played well, and they turned the long street with its blazing shop-windows and its shining lamps and its gleaming cars into a setting for carnival. Just to listen was to feel suddenly uplifted and happy.

Behind them were two men carrying a huge white banner on which was written in tall black letters: RELEASE STEVE ANDERSON, and behind them a snowstorm of smaller placards and posters: IS THIS DEMOCRACY?; STEVE FOR PRIME MINISTER; FREEDOM TO SAY NO. As the music passed, then the banner, I began to hear the chant of those that followed: Steve OUT! Steve OUT! Steve OUT!

And I remembered Steve Anderson, the pacifist: he who had written articles denouncing the United Nations, the Americans, the Russians, the Chinese and not least his own country. He who had fasted for ten days, his sleeping-bag pitched by the Artillery Memorial at Hyde Park Corner, alongside the dead and shrouded metal soldier whose face was hidden under a metal greatcoat, and whose hard fingers often grasped a few dying flowers. He who had led demonstrations at Holy Loch, and the Germ Warfare Centre somewhere in Wiltshire; and who had finally been arrested when he had smashed a dozen or so display-cases at the Imperial War Museum, and who was now awaiting the result of his Appeal.

It is difficult to describe how I felt. Happy yes, excited yes, my own latent enthusiasm mirrored in the faces, the shouts, the music, the laughter. And when from a group of flag-wavers came a shout of *Don't just stand there — come on!* I ran forward and became part of the parade.

'Where are you going?' I said to the girl who wore a college scarf.

'Downing Street,' she said. 'We're going to demand to see someone — and present a petition.'

'Where did you start?'

'Hammersmith,' she said. 'You wait till we get to Trafalgar Square. Another lot's joining us there.'

And before long I too was shouting Steve OUT! Steve OUT! as we marched past Kensington Gardens, Hyde Park Corner, down Piccadilly, the Haymarket — and into the Square.

They were there, near the lions — another hundred or so, with another group playing. It was marvellous. Together we set off down Whitehall.

It was obvious that the police had been forewarned. They stretched right across the road at the entrance to Downing Street. Behind them the blue steel of the cans, the winking lights of their cars, the nasal crackling of their radios.

Gradually the procession lost its narrowness as the demonstrators surged forward to press against the double-ranked line of policemen. An inspector spoke from the pavement, the loud-hailer bouncing his words off the tall buildings, their echo sounding far off towards the river.

'That's enough, then,' he said. 'Keep it orderly, please. I understand you have a petition. Three of you can present it. Come forward please. The rest will disperse after it's been presented.'

'Not likely,' a man called out near me. 'We're coming, too. Let him see how many there are.'

'Yes,' shouted the crowd. 'Downing Street, Downing Street.'

This was repeated all the way back. Near the front, I found myself being pushed closer to the ranks of blue. I also began to feel a little scared. There were too many of us. I couldn't move anywhere but forward. The music had stopped, and all there was now was a mass of crushed and heaving bodies, gradually gathering its strength to break out.

'Will the organizers of this demonstration speak to these people please,' said the inspector. 'Only those presenting the petition can enter the street.

Will they come forward.'

By now I was among the first of the crowd, and it was from my position in the front that I saw two men and a woman step out from the centre, the woman holding two large envelopes.

'Are you the petition-party?' said the inspector.

'Yes.'

'Let them through. And *only* them.'

But he was too late. As a few policemen stepped back, so the mass behind me, seeing its chance, rushed forward. Like a piece of driftwood on the tip of a wave I found myself hurled against the uniform immediately in front of me. The man gasped, tried vainly to link arms with his companions on either side, failed and fell back. I panicked now, feeling all humanity at my back. Clear sharp flashes of fear: wide eyes, breaths, open mouths, hands grasping, curses, laughter, shock and fright at sudden pain. There was a clear space in front of me, and I ran like a hare seeing the wide field open up. Straight into the inspector. The loud-hailer fell from his hand with a clatter and, winded, he clutched at me. As he did so, our equal force knocked the book out of my hand, and it flew to the gutter like a broken-backed bird.

'My book!' I said. 'My book!'

Furious, he still held me.

'You stay still, my girl. Or else.'

I saw out of the corner of my eye the crowd

surging forward. Soon the book would be trampled on, destroyed, finished.

'Oh, let me go! Let me go!'

But his grip increased as he shouted orders to his men. Incensed, there was only one thing I could do. I lifted my foot and kicked him hard in the ankle. I had on my sandals with the wooden soles, and it must have hurt. I felt my own toes jar with the force.

He gave one loud choked-down cry, and released me.

I managed to snatch the book before the crowd reached it. But he also recovered quickly and, limping forward, made sure I was secure this time.

I was the first to be placed in the van.

About twenty of us were arrested. At the station we sat together on a long bench, and were called forward one by one to give details at the desk. When it was my turn a sergeant whispered to the constable who was asking the questions.

'So you're the one who crocked the inspector, are you?' said the constable. 'Shot at dawn, you'll be.'

'Or given a medal,' said the sergeant.

The constable laughed.

'Right,' he said. 'Name?'

'Katie Gilson.'

'Your real name, mind.'

'Is it that funny?' I said. I was mad and fed up.

The spine of the book had become detached: it was ruined. And now this. 'Oh, I suppose you want the other one. Katie Morris, now.'

He snorted.

'That's better. Age?'

'Sixteen.'

'Address?'

I gave it, and the telephone number.

'Are your parents at home?'

'No.'

He looked up from the form.

'No?'

'They're on holiday in Bournemouth.'

'Are they now? You on your own? At home?'

'Yes.'

He clicked his tongue.

'I don't know,' he said: 'call themselves parents.'

'It was my own choice.'

'No doubt, no doubt,' he said. 'Well, their holiday will have to be interrupted, won't it? What address in Bournemouth?'

'Why?'

'They'll have to come and collect you. That's why. On the phone, are they? Friends? Hotel?'

'Oh, don't do that,' I said. 'Just let me go and I'll . . .'

'You're lucky you're not going to be charged with assaulting an officer of the law,' said the sergeant. 'No, they'll have to come and get you. It's time these parents of yours learned what you kids get up to. Now, where are they staying?'

'I'm not going to tell you.'

'You'll only have to stay the night,' he said, and he made a face, as if it were a terrifying prospect. But I favoured that, rather than dragging them all the way up to town again. I recalled Miss O'Dell suddenly: it was all experience.

'Lock me up, then,' I said. 'Where's the cell?'

He sighed.

'Go and sit down, Joan of Arc,' he said.

It didn't take them long. I suppose it was easy to ring the hotels. I should have stuck to Katie Gilson. It would have taken longer.

But the sergeant looked serious when he beckoned me over to the desk at about eleven o'clock.

'Go in that room over there, will you? Yes, there.'

He followed me in a few minutes later, and waved me to a chair.

'I've sent for a cup of tea,' he said. 'And a bite of something.'

'Thank you.'

He sat down behind the table.

'I've just been speaking to your mother,' he said. He rubbed a finger against his nose. 'She's just about had enough of you.'

'Oh?'

'She's not coming up to collect you. She says what you need is a good sharp shock to bring you to your senses. What do you think about that?'

There was a knock at the door, and a cup of tea and a slice of currant-cake were placed in front of me.

'No sugar,' I said.

'Better than bread and water. Well, what do you think about that?'

I felt the last of her need for me, and mine of her, fall away like the slow uncoiling of a rope.

'It's understandable,' I said. 'I don't care.'

He remained silent, turning the biro over in his fingers.

'If she refuses to collect you and doesn't want anything to do with you — you know what that means?'

I sipped the sour tea.

'Prison?'

'Not that bad,' he said. 'It means we'll have to remand you until we decide what's best. What do you think about that?'

'It's all experience.'

He leaned back in the chair.

'So what we're going to do is take you to a remand home, and you'll be seen in court tomorrow.'

If he expected tears, he wasn't going to get any. I munched the cake and swallowed the last of the tea.

'All right,' I said. 'You do that.'

I think I half-wanted to see her in the courtroom, hear her say she wanted me back. But she did not come.

After a night in the remand home, in a small bare room and on a hard bed, I woke tired but not desperate. I think all the time I was more worried about the book. Its condition seemed infinitely more important than my own.

Anyway, Miss Roberts, you probably know the result. She did not come, and I was remanded again for a week *while inquiries are made*. From the court a policewoman took me home, and watched me pack a few personal things. We were back at about twelve-thirty, a little before lunch.

It was here, in the dining-hall, across a long formica-topped table, that I met Grace Darling — the girl with whom I was to share another room.

9

My first impression of Grace was one of colour and vitality. Since we were on remand we were allowed our own clothes, and she took full advantage of the fact. Her hair was very fair and hung loosely about her shoulders, framing a face which was very tanned and which bore little make-up. She was wearing a plain white blouse open at the throat, and round her neck she had tied a brilliant red scarf: looking rather like a cow-girl in a Western musical. Below the blouse a gold-buckled belt held a skirt two or three shades darker than her scarf.

Her first sentence was none too welcoming.

'You the Morris kid?'

Kid! We were about the same age.

'I'm Katie Morris. Yes.'

'You're sharing with me. Right? My name's Grace Darling. And before we go any further I don't want any cracks about lifeboats, lighthouses, storms, seas or rescues. Understand? Once we get that settled we can go ahead. Pass the salt.'

'How long have you been here?' I said.

'About a week,' she said. 'A week tomorrow. I'm

remanded for medical reports. I've had two sessions with a nutter, and another coming up tomorrow morning. But don't get worried. I'm not the violent type.'

'What did you do?'

'Lots of things they don't know about,' she said. 'I'll tell you later. My turn to get the pudding.'

After she had emptied the tray she came and sat down again.

'And what did *you* do?' she said.

I told her.

'Poor old you,' she said. 'Your mother's not up to much, then?'

Surprisingly enough, I found myself defending her.

'She's not too bad,' I said. 'She had a lot to do — putting up with me.'

Grace smiled, her spoon half-way to her mouth.

'My mother's lovely,' she said. 'You'll have to come and see her when we're out.'

This was the second aspect of Grace which endeared her to me: her complete and utter openness to other people. Not for a moment did she consider that I might not wish to meet her mother, or to know herself once we had separated.

'She thinks I'm mad — my mother,' she said. '*Grace,* she says, *what did I ever do to deserve you?*'

'What about your father?'

'Oh, he's given up. He just looks bewildered most of the time. You met the boss yet?'

'Who?'

'Mrs. Gordon and her band of merry helpers.'

'No.'

'That'll be this afternoon, I suppose. She's not bad. Says the usual things. All you have to do is agree. It keeps them happy and they think they're getting somewhere. Mind you, what you think underneath is your own business. Finished? Let's go outside. We've got a quarter of an hour.'

Between the main building and the high wall was a long stretch of garden: a few wooden seats scattered about, sounds of the city, a chitter of visiting sparrows. We sat down.

'I love the sun,' she said. 'Used to peel like anything when I was a kid. Not now.' She reached up her hands as if to touch the sky. 'Can't get enough of it. Ever been to a psychiatrist, Katie?'

'No.'

'Very interesting cases, they are.'

She laughed out loud.

'They're so interested in wanting you normal,' she said. 'Who's normal?' She draped her arm over the back of the seat. 'Are you normal, Katie?'

'No.'

'Of course not. There's more out than in.'

'You haven't told me what you've done.'

'Guess.'

I looked at her, and could think of no crime that fitted the slightly mocking face beside me.

'Shop-lifting?'

'How dare you,' she said. 'No. Guess again.'

'Er . . . I don't know really.'

'I went swimming in the Serpentine.'

'Not only that, surely.'

'That's all. Mind you, I didn't wear a swimming-costume.'

'Well . . .'

'And it was after midnight.'

'Well . . .'

'*And* with a crowd of others. And, let me whisper it, Katie — some were boys. See, you're shocked already. *And* it was the second time. Once before in St. James' Park lake. About two in the morning. Big moon. Ducks waking up all round us. Marvellous.'

'Wasn't it cold?'

'We've had some warm nights lately. Or haven't you noticed? Anyway, it couldn't be normal, could it? Frightening the ducks like that? And my mum said I was beyond her control, poor old thing. I told her — that's what comes of getting married too late. You know how old my mum was when she had me? Nearly fifty! She went to the doctor's for some advice on slimming — and it was *me*!'

She laughed again, that rich open-mouthed throat-back laugh.

'Can you beat it?' she said.

'You're not still at school?' I said.

'No, are you? Got any Levels yet?'

'One A, two Os.'

'I've only got one O,' she said. 'Domestic Science. Make a lovely lemon meringue, I do. Couldn't better it at the Dorchester, I bet.'

'Have you got a job?'

'Had a few,' she said. 'Marks and Sparks. Stamping prices on baked-bean tins. Tried an office once — filing, all that. But it's not life, is it? Same time, same spot on the dial — not life. Not for me. Isn't this sun glorious? Mm. Now wouldn't it be nice to be on some beach now, soaking it all in?'

'You have to have money,' I said.

'That's the trouble. You know, once at our school we had a visiting vicar or something. You know — the good word, and all that. Know what he said? *All the gold you want is within you*. I thought of saying *That may satisfy you, mate, but not me*.'

A bell rang high on the brick wall.

'See you at tea,' she said. 'Always answer the bell on the dot. Keeps them happy.'

That afternoon, as she had predicted, I had my interview with Mrs. Gordon; and I took Grace's advice and agreed to everything: that I was not treating my mother fairly; that I had to pull myself together or I would be a loss to society, etcetera, etcetera.

I spent the rest of the afternoon helping in the kitchen. Grace was there, and as we worked among the flour and the pastry and the pie-dishes we talked — or, rather, she did.

'Happy?' she said, using the glass rolling-pin. 'How can you be happy if you've not got your freedom? No, like I said — you've got to make the most of it. After all, what's going to happen the day after tomorrow? They'll have these reports from the nutters, and they'll say *Grace Darling is just a high-spirited lass* — I mean, what else can they say, I haven't done anything really wrong. It'll be probation, won't it? And then, while the sun shines . . . Oh, my mother will take me back. She always does. She'll be in court and she'll put her little hankie to her eyes and say *Oh she's a good girl, really, sir, just a bit head-strong, like I was when I was a girl* — and all the old grey-wigs will nod. And I'll be out in the open, and away. What are you looking down in the mouth for?'

'I was thinking about my mother.'

'She might come round. They usually do.'

'I wasn't thinking that way. Still, perhaps it's too late.'

She grinned and expertly cut the pastry around the dish.

'It's never too late,' she said.

At least she was right about her own case. I

watched her go off on Friday morning, and by lunchtime she was back for her clothes. We met in the hall. Beside her was a small, crushed-looking woman with marks of recent tears under a dusting of powder.

'What did I tell you?' said Grace. 'On probation for a year. Mum, this is Katie.'

'I don't know where she gets it from,' said Mrs. Darling. 'Not from me or her father — that I do know. And what are you here for, love?'

'She robbed a bank, didn't you, Katie? Got away with six thousand, Mum.'

'I don't believe it,' said her mother.

Grace bent down and kissed the top of her head.

'Isn't she lovely, Katie? Told you she'd take me back, didn't I?'

'But not for long, my girl — if you don't try harder. You play me up once more and I'll see that probation officer and . . .'

'Yes, Mum, of course you will.'

'Can we go now?' said Mrs. Darling. 'I can't say I like this place.'

'Yes, let's be out of it,' said Grace. She kissed me. 'So long, Katie. See you outside. I liked those talks in the garden. I'll write — or something.'

'Goodbye,' I said.

I watched them walk down the main hall,

escorted by one of the staff. Then I went into lunch.

The place seemed dull now that she had gone, and by Saturday morning, waking alone in the large room, wondering who was going to share it with me in the next few days, I felt decidedly fed up.

But there was a letter for me after breakfast. It was from Miss O'Dell. I had written to her about the book.

Dear Katie,

I was appalled to hear your story, and to hear where you are. I can well imagine what your mother must be feeling. I read about the demonstration, but hardly thought that you were involved. Please don't worry too much about the book. It's sad, but it's not the end of the world. Perhaps we can repair it when next we meet. If there is anything I can do to help, please let me know. And please write often. If you can.

Yours sincerely,

Georgina (Richard) O'Dell

It was a load off my mind. I *had* repaired it as best I could, using some gummed linen-tape the library-officer had given me, but for some reason I had not been able to settle to read it. With her letter in my hand, at last I felt I could make a second attempt.

That afternoon was to be spent in games and, later on, a film was to be shown. After lunch I went out into the garden again and sat on the same bench Grace and I had shared. Sitting there listlessly, the book unopened in my lap, I heard a sudden clunk on the ground behind me, and looking over my shoulder I saw a piece of weighted paper rolling to a standstill near the lettuces. I looked around. No one else had noticed it, or was paying any attention to my part of the garden. I stood up and strolled slowly across the gravel, bent down as if to fix my shoe, and picked up the paper. I unwrapped the stone, let it drop among others and smoothed out the message.

K,

Come to the laundry-gate. Now.

G

The laundry-gate was a tall, heavily-studded double door at the end of the garden, topped by shards of glass and a twist of barbed-wire. Trucks used it for deliveries. It was a kind of tradesmen's entrance, separate from the main gate.

I walked slowly towards it and leaned my back against the studs. It creaked.

'That you, Katie?' said Grace, from the street.

'Yes.'

'What a fizz, eh?'

'Hallo, Katie,' said another, much louder voice.

'Shut up!' she said.

'Who's that?'

'Tim,' she said. 'Trust you to spoil it, dope.'

He laughed.

'Sorry. Look through the crack, Katie. Let's see what you look like.'

'She can't,' said Grace. 'Anyway, she can't stay long. Katie?'

'Yes?'

'Do you want to be on this side?'

'Of course I do.'

'Well, I've been thinking. It's easy. You've got the film at the usual time? Seven?'

'Yes.'

'Well, half-way through say you're not feeling very well, and go to the San and get an aspirin or that stomach-settler stuff.'

'Why?'

'Wait a minute and I'll tell you. Then, while you're there ask to go to the lav. You know the nurse there — big one? Well, it doesn't matter if you don't. Anyway, she's pretty easy, and . . . Are you listening?'

'Yes,' I said. 'But hurry up. Aggie's coming this way.'

'Oh. Well, don't go to the lav. Go along the corridor to the right and there's a room where they keep the brooms and stuff. I had to help there once. There's a window inside — I can just see it from here. It's always open. Get through and . . .'

'I'll be there,' said Tim. 'I'll help you down, Katie sweet.'

'Okay?' said Grace. 'Just after eight?'

'Aggie's seen me,' I said.

'We'll be there, anyway,' said Grace. 'See you.'

'Morris!' called Aggie.

'Yes?'

'Here. And quickly.'

I pushed myself off the studs and walked towards her.

'You're not to go to games this afternoon,' she said. 'Mrs. Gordon wants to see you at two-thirty in her office. So stay in your room until then.'

'Why? What's . . .?'

'You just be there at two-thirty sharp. And don't hang around here. Back into the garden.'

Until two-thirty I lay on my bed and read *Evaline*. Or tried to. But the thought of Grace kept recurring. In imagination I was already there, balancing on slates or bricks, wet with a summer rainstorm, the tall boy with the damp, flattened hair reaching out, wet fingers grasping, slipping . . . All the images from escape-stories. Part of me knew I would sit through the film and never make a move; but another part — the part that loved the wild, uncaring freedom of Grace and her kind — told that other conventional me that here was a chance to inhabit another life. But what kind of life? That was the trouble.

At dead on two-thirty I was outside the boss's room, tapping at the brown panels.

'Come in.'

The first shock was seeing my mother in the chair near the filing-cabinet. She made no effort to greet me, but smiled uncertainly, unsure of my reaction.

'Would you like to say hello to your mother?' said Mrs. Gordon.

It was I who was uncertain now, but the custom of years cannot be erased that easily. I put my hands on her shoulders and kissed her.

'Good. Now come and sit down.'

I sat opposite her, the afternoon sun in my eyes.

'Katie, your mother contacted me yesterday and we had a long talk. She feels that you've had a sufficiently hard time of it, and she wants you back.'

I did not look in her direction.

'How do you feel about that?'

'I don't know,' I said. 'I'm not certain any more. I . . .'

'Well you see, my dear, if you don't agree, the court can only find you in need of care and protection — and that will mean an approved school.'

Defeated, I could say nothing.

'If you agree, I could get you home very quickly, Katie. Perhaps even on Monday.'

I could still think of nothing to say. Then I thought of Grace. Supposing that I did . . .? But my mother broke my thoughts.

'Tell her the other possibility,' she said.

Mrs. Gordon looked at her.

'Now, Mrs. Morris, I thought we agreed . . .'

'Tell her,' said my mother.

'Well, Katie, there *is* something else. The courts have always wanted to help intelligent girls — girls of above-average intelligence, that is — and I discussed this with your mother yesterday. Of course, if you'd rather go home . . .'

'Please tell her,' said my mother. 'Let her choose.'

'Have you heard anyone speak of *The Grange* while you've been here, Katie?'

'No, Mrs. Gordon.'

'Well, it's the first of its kind, Katie, and it's in Norfolk. It's more a college than a hostel; and it's for helping people like you: intelligent girls who have gone off the rails a little. Now, your mother has spoken a great deal about your literary ability, the A and O Levels you've been awarded; and, plus the fact of your good behaviour here — well, I've been in touch with Mrs. Talbot, and providing the court agrees, you could go there as soon as possible: the new term starts in another week. But I'm certain you'd rather go home.'

'Let her choose,' said my mother again.

This time I looked at her. And, with a sudden flash of gratitude, I saw that what she was offering me was a kind of freedom. Freely given, out of love.

'You could take your other Levels there,' said my mother. 'It's in the country. It'd be a change — help you to sort yourself out. And I'll always be here. At home.'

'Well, what do you think?' said Mrs. Gordon.

'How long would I have to stay there?'

'At the most until you were eighteen,' said Mrs. Gordon. 'A lot sooner, if you liked. You'd be very lucky, Katie.'

I sat there, my eyes half-closed in the sun. Thinking of Grace.

'All right,' I said. 'Yes.'

'That's settled then,' said Mrs. Gordon. 'Now, I'll just leave you to have a few words with your mother. You could make a list together of the things you'd need.'

The door closed behind her.

We stood there like statues. It was she who made the first move.

'Katie dear,' she said. 'I'm sorry. But you *were* naughty.'

The use of the infant word made me want to laugh and cry at the same time.

'How's everyone?' I said.

'Oh, all right. I do miss you, Katie. You were a silly girl.'

'Shall we make that list? And what about the school?'

'Katie,' she said. 'Look at me. I wanted to come, and yet I didn't. Jack said time and time again *Come on, I'll drive you*. But I just couldn't — I was so hurt, Katie. I lay there all night, not a wink of sleep. You've not stopped loving me, have you?'

'You shouldn't ask questions like that,' I said. 'It's not fair. Let's make the list.'

The first film that evening was a cartoon: the usual cat chasing the usual mouse.

Then the big one began. It was very old, the picture grubby with age, the voices bubbling as though they spoke under water.

On the wall at the end of my row was a large brown-faced clock, and in the half-darkness I could just make out the time.

At ten to eight I stood up, moved along against the knees and the occasional joker who tried to trip me, and went to the officer on duty.

'Why?' said Aggie.

'I don't feel at all well,' I said. 'I think it was that Welsh Rarebit — too greasy for me.'

She looked around.

'I'll have to find someone to go with you.'

'Oh, it doesn't matter,' I said. 'You can trust me.'

'You're the one who's going to *The Grange*, aren't you? Well, hop along then. Come straight back.'

It was still light outside, but the first stars were budding in the evening sky.

The tall nurse was on duty, and after I had drunk the chalky, peppermint mixture, I was given permission to use the lavatory. I found the broom-store easy enough, and after clambering over pails and mops and brushes I reached the open window and looked out. A flat roof was immediately underneath, then a gap of about a foot and then the outer wall.

'Tim,' I whispered.

After a while his hands appeared, then his head.

'Great,' he said softly. 'Get out and come over.' He looked down into the street. 'Yes, she's here.' Then he looked back at me. 'Come on.'

The slight breeze lifted the points of his shirt-collar, beating.

'Tell Grace I'm sorry,' I said. 'I'm not coming.'

'What?'

'I'm not coming. Get down quickly, before someone sees you.'

'Just a minute,' he said.

He disappeared. And then struggling to the top came Grace, slipping as she tried to steady herself.

'Come on, Katie,' she said. 'What's all this about? You've come this far.'

'I can't. I'm sorry.'

'Why not?'

'I . . . I just can't. Go before you get into trouble.'

She grinned.

'Oh, come on, Kate. We're going down to Brighton. Tim's got a friend. And a car.'

'I'm sorry,' I said. 'Good luck.'

She looked at me and shook her head.

'You don't know what you're missing. Cheerio, semi-detached.'

She dropped from the wall, and I heard the car drive off as I quietly closed the door behind me.

The film was still on, still old, still bubbling.

'Hallo,' said Aggie. 'Better now?'

10

Well, Miss Roberts, you know the rest. The court agreed; and Miss Evans, who comes from Norwich and was due for leave anyway, brought me this far, and handed me over. To you — and your stupid assignment.

I suppose in a way I should be grateful. Writing this has kept me occupied, safe from running over the flat fields . . . to what?

But, of course, you will never read it. For what you wanted was handed in the following evening: two pages of pupil-to-teacher semi-truths and downright lies. I gave you what you expected: helped you fix the label. You were childishly pleased. Even commented on a few *poetic sentences* in the next tutorial. Good for you.

No, I didn't write this for you, Miss Roberts. Perhaps for my mother — that she might understand. Perhaps for the memory of Eva Stewart and rain-marked doves and open books made of marble. Most probably for Richard O'Dell and the small woman who bears his name. Perhaps for you, Grace, sleeping rough on whatever moonlit beach tonight.

But mostly, I suppose, for myself.

more TOPLINERS for your enjoyment

by E. W. HILDICK
Birdy in Amsterdam
The canals of Amsterdam lead Birdy into deep water

by ROY WILSON
First Season
Life is tough for Danny before he makes the big time in football

by DIANNE DOUBTFIRE
Escape on Monday
Veronica and her mother begin to understand each other after a dramatic conflict over Veronica's boy friend, Terry

edited by AIDAN CHAMBERS
I Want To Get Out
An anthology of prose and poetry by teenage writers

by CHRISTOPHER LEACH
Decision for Katie
Katie finds that looking after Graham involves more than she imagined

by PAUL ZINDEL
The Pigman
Life is simple for a generous old man until he meets two American teenagers

compiled by AIDAN and NANCY CHAMBERS
World Zero Minus: An S. F. Anthology
An exciting collection of science-fiction stories

TOPLINERS published by Macmillan

more TOPLINERS for your enjoyment

compiled by AIDAN and NANCY CHAMBERS
Ghosts
An anthology of stories of the supernatural definitely Not to be Taken at Bedtime

by AIDAN CHAMBERS
Ghosts II
More spine-chilling stories of the supernatural

by HONOR ARUNDEL
The Girl in the Opposite Bed
Jane hates being in hospital but by the time she goes home she knows much more about people – herself as well as others

by INGER BRATTSTROM
Since That Party
Odd-man-out Nicholas, who adores popular Stella from afar, gives a birthday party . . . with unforeseeable consequences

and many other titles – send to the publishers for a complete list.

The editor of Topliners is always pleased to hear what readers think of the books and to receive ideas for new titles. If you want to write to him please address your letter to: The Editor, Topliners, Macmillan, Houndmills, Basingstoke, Hampshire. All letters received will be answered.

TOPLINERS published by Macmillan